BASIC COSTING

Qualifications and Credit Framework

Level 2 Certificate in Accounting

British Library Cataloguing-in-Publication Data

A catalogue record for this book is available from the British Library.

Published by
Kaplan Publishing UK
Unit 2, The Business Centre
Molly Millars Lane
Wokingham
Berkshire
RG41 2QZ

ISBN 978-0-85732-593-8

Printed and bound in Great Britain.

We are grateful to the Association of Accounting Technicians for permission to reproduce past assessment materials and example tasks based on the new syllabus. The solutions to past answers and similar activities in the style of the new syllabus have been prepared by Kaplan Publishing.

CONTENTS

STUDY TEXT AND WORKBOOK

INTRODUCTION

HOW TO USE THESE MATERIALS

These Kaplan Publishing learning materials have been carefully designed to make your learning experience as easy as possible and to give you the best chance of success in your AAT assessments.

They contain a number of features to help you in the study process.

The sections on the Unit Guide, the Assessment and Study Skills should be read before you commence your studies.

They are designed to familiarise you with the nature and content of the assessment and to give you tips on how best to approach your studies.

STUDY TEXT

This study text has been specially prepared for the revised AAT qualification introduced in July 2010.

It is written in a practical and interactive style:

- key terms and concepts are clearly defined

- all topics are illustrated with practical examples with clearly worked solutions based on sample tasks provided by the AAT in the new examining style

- frequent practice activities throughout the chapters ensure that what you have learnt is regularly reinforced

- 'pitfalls' and 'examination tips' help you avoid commonly made mistakes and help you focus on what is required to perform well in your examination

- practice workbook activities can be completed at the end of each chapter

WORKBOOK

The workbook comprises:

Practice activities at the end of each chapter with solutions at the end of the text, to reinforce the work covered in each chapter.

The questions are divided into their relevant chapters and students may either attempt these questions as they work through the textbook, or leave some or all of these until they have completed the textbook as a final revision of what they have studied.

ICONS

The study chapters include the following icons throughout.

They are designed to assist you in your studies by identifying key definitions and the points at which you can test yourself on the knowledge gained.

Definition

These sections explain important areas of Knowledge which must be understood and reproduced in an assessment

Example

The illustrative examples can be used to help develop an understanding of topics before attempting the activity exercises

Activity

These are exercises which give the opportunity to assess your understanding of all the assessment areas.

UNIT GUIDE

Basic Costing is divided into two units but for the purposes of assessment these units will be combined.

Basic Principles of Costing (Knowledge)

4 credits

Providing Basic Cost and Revenue Information (Skills)

2 credits

Purpose of the units

The creation of these two core units at level two recognises the need to build a sound foundation in costing to give the candidate the relevant knowledge and skills to take forward to the more complex costing and management accounting units they will study at levels 3 and 4. At the same time candidates are made aware of the importance of the costing system as a source of information for internal management decision making as contrasted with financial accounting which looks outwards.

Learning objectives

The Basic Principles of Costing unit requires candidates to have an underlying knowledge and understanding of the nature of a cost accounting system within an organisation and its component parts as well as an understanding of how it operates.

The Provide Basic Cost and Revenue Information unit allows candidates to demonstrate the skills they have acquired in using the cost system to record or extract data and providing information on actual and expected costs.

It should be stressed that these two units provide an introduction to costing and are looking to develop basic skills that the candidate will build upon in later studies.

On completion of these units the learner will be able to:

- Understand the nature of stock at its different stages in the production process; learners will be expected to be familiar with the components of a manufacturing account

- Identify the characteristics of FIFO, LIFO and AVCO as methods of stock valuation and cost an issue and value closing stock by each method

- Identify labour cost by nature (direct or indirect)

- Identify the characteristics of time rate, piecework and time rate with bonus as methods of labour remuneration

- Calculate and explain labour remuneration using the above methods

- Understand what is a variance and calculate a variance by comparing actual cost with budgeted cost

- Identify whether a variance is adverse or favourable

- Identify whether a variance is significant and the manager to whom this should be reported

Learning Outcomes and Assessment criteria

Each unit consists of two learning outcomes, each comprising of a number of assessment criteria

Basic Principles of Costing (Knowledge)

1   Demonstrate an understanding of the cost recording system within an organisation

2   Recognise the component parts of a cost recording system and how this operates

Provide Basic Cost and Revenue Information (Skills)

1   Use the cost recording system to record or extract data

2   Provide information on actual and expected costs.

KAPLAN PUBLISHING

Knowledge

To perform this unit effectively you will need to know and understand the following:

		Chapter
1	**Demonstrate and understanding of the cost recording system within an organisation**	
1.1	Explain the nature of the organisation's business transactions in relation to its accounting systems	1
1.2	Explain the purpose and structure of a costing system within an organisation	1
1.3	Describe the relationships between the costing and accounting systems within the organisation	1
1.4	Identify sources of income and expenditure information for historic, current and forecast periods	All
2	**Recognise the component parts of a cost recording system and how this operates**	
2.1	Identify materials, labour and expenses and explain how they are classified and recorded	3,4
2.2	Explain fixed variable and semi-variable overheads	1
2.3	Identify types of cost and profit centres	1
2.4	Explain different methods of coding data	2
2.5	Identify different types of stock: raw materials, part-finished goods (work-in-progress), finished goods	3
2.6	Explain different methods of stock valuation	3
2.7	Explain methods for calculating payments for labour	4

Skills

To perform this unit effectively you will need to be able to do the following.

Chapter

1   **Use the cost recording system to record or extract data**

1.1	Identify or clarify information requirements	1
1.2	Extract income and expenditure details from relevant sources.	1,2
1.3	Distinguish between fixed, variable and semi-variable overheads	1
1.4	Classify, calculate and code cost information for materials, labour and expenses	1,2
1.5	Calculate stock valuations using appropriate methods	3

2   **Provide information on actual and expected costs**

2.1	Compare actual and expected costs.	5
2.2	Identify any discrepancies and refer or report to an appropriate person	5

Delivery guidance

The AAT have provided delivery guidance giving further details of the way in which the unit will be assessed.

Delivery Guidance: Basic Principles of Costing

1.   Demonstrate and understanding of the cost recording system within an organisation

1.1   Explain the nature of the organisation's business transactions in relation to its accounting systems

Candidates need to understand what constitutes cost in different organisations. For instance a cost structure within a manufacturing industry will be different from a cost structure within a service industry and so the costing systems will differ. Candidates will be required to identify the elements of cost (materials, labour, and overheads) within an organisation and the nature of the cost (direct or indirect)

KAPLAN PUBLISHING

1.2 Explain the purpose and structure of a costing system within an organisation

Candidates must develop an understanding of what a costing system brings to an organisation. In order to do this they must be able to classify cost by element, nature and behaviour (fixed, variable or semi-variable). From this the candidate must be able to explain the purpose and role of the costing system in particular determining product cost and hence selling price, valuing stock, providing information for financial statements and management decision making

1.3 Describe the relationships between the costing and accounting systems within the organisation

Candidates must understand the nature of the costing and accounting systems within the organisation. This requires knowledge of their purpose and what they are trying to achieve. Essential to this is the need to understand how each system uses cost; the costing system dependent upon the information that is required for it (product cost will need cost classified by element) contrasted with the accounting system which will require cost classified by function (production, administration, selling and distribution etc)

1.4 Identify sources of income and expenditure information for historic, current and forecast periods

Candidates must be able to identify how financial accounts are used to provide data for historic periods, how actual or estimated materials and labour costs and estimated overheads are used, for instance, to arrive at a job cost for the current period, and how budgeted costs are used for forecast periods

2. Recognise the component parts of a cost recording system and how this operates

2.1 Identify materials, labour and expenses and explain how they are classified and recorded

Candidates must be able to identify, classify and record across a range of business organisations materials, labour and expenses as either direct or indirect; fixed or variable

2.2 Explain fixed variable and semi-variable overheads

Candidates must be able to define what overheads are and be able to classify their behaviour as fixed, variable or semi-variable. Candidates will be required to classify overhead costs under one of these headings and be able to give examples of such classification.

2.3 Identify types of cost and profit centres

Candidates will be expected to understand what is meant by a cost centre and profit centre, why they are used in a costing system and be able to classify a given centre appropriately

2.4 Explain different methods of coding data

Candidates must be able to explain and understand a range of coding systems (numeric, alphabetic, alpha-numeric). Candidates must be able to identify a given coding system method from its description.

2.5 Identify different types of stock: raw materials, part-finished goods (work-in-progress), finished goods

Candidates must understand the flow of stock through the stages of manufacture and be able to identify the components of a cost statement for manufactured goods appreciating the classification of stock in arriving at prime cost, factory cost and cost of production of goods sold.

2.6 Explain different methods of stock valuation

Candidates must be able to explain FIFO, LIFO and AVCO as methods of valuing raw material stock and understand how they operate. Candidates will not be required to compare methods.

2.7 Explain methods for calculating payments for labour

Candidates will be required to understand and explain methods of payment for labour to include basic rate (time rate), payment of overtime, payment of bonus, payment by piecework. Candidates will not be required to have knowledge of specific bonus schemes.

Delivery Guidance: Provide Basic Cost and Revenue Information

1. Use the cost recording system to record or extract data

1.1 Identify or clarify information requirements

Candidates will be expected to identify information requirements relating to costs and income. For instance when requested by managers to show how unit cost behaves be able to present unit costs for different levels of output. Candidates will have to be aware of the relevant managers significance reports will be sent to.

1.2 Extract income and expenditure details from relevant sources.

Relevant sources will include purchase invoices, purchase orders, sales invoices, and payroll. Candidates will be required to extract this information and use it for management information purposes.

1.3   Distinguish between fixed, variable and semi-variable overheads

Candidates will be expected to use the knowledge base they have developed to calculate unit cost over a range of output levels when given variable cost per unit and total fixed costs. Candidates will also be expected to determine total costs for a new production level when given information about total costs for different production levels.

1.4   Classify, calculate and code cost information for materials, labour and expenses

Candidates will be expected to use their knowledge base of cost classification to classify cost information by element (materials, labour and expenses) Candidates could be expected to calculate these elements of cost and then code them using a policy manual that will be given.

1.5   Calculate stock valuations using appropriate methods

Candidates will be expected to be able to value an issue of stock from the stores department to the production department using FIFO, LIFO and AVCO and calculate closing stock using each method.

2.   Provide information on actual and expected costs

2.1   Compare actual and expected costs.

Candidates will be required to understand that expected costs could be budgeted costs. A brief knowledge of budgeting as an aid to planning and control is expected but this needs only to be at a basic level. Candidates will not be required to explain the nature of budgeted costs in any great detail, but will be required to identify budgeted costs and to compare with actual costs.

2.2   Identify any discrepancies and refer or report to an appropriate person

Candidates should be able to understand the difference between actual and expected cost as being a variance. Candidates should know what is meant by a favourable variance and an adverse variance and be able to calculate what the variance is. Again this is at a basic level and the only calculation required will be a comparison of actual to expected cost.

Candidates should note that discrepancies are variances above a certain %. Candidates must be able to determine such variances by comparing actual cost and expected cost calculating the variance as either a positive (favourable) or negative (adverse) amount and then expressing as a %. This is the only variance calculation. There is no calculation of sub-variances and no need to apply any formulae to the calculation.

Candidates should be able to identify to whom the variance report should be sent to (the appropriate person). This means the candidate should be aware of the reporting structure in the organisation and that material variances might want to be seen by the production manager and purchasing manager, labour variances might want to be seen by the production manager and HR manager, and expense variances might want to be seen by the administration manager. The reasons why these managers would want to see these variances and the causes of the variances are not required.

THE ASSESSMENT

The format of the assessment

The assessment will be divided into two sections.

Section 1:

Section 1 will be principally knowledge based and will cover

- Cost identification and coding
- Cost behaviour
- Structure of a product cost

Expect to see 12 tasks in section 1.

Section 2:

Section 2 will be principally skill based and will cover

- Costing for Stock and Work-in-Progress (Inventories)
- Costing for labour
- Budgeting

Expect to see 14 tasks in section 2.

Learners will normally be assessed by computer based assessment (CBA), which will include extended writing tasks, and will be required to demonstrate competence in both sections of the assessment.

For the purpose of assessment the competency level for AAT assessment is set at 70 per cent.

Time allowed

The time allowed for this assessment is **120 minutes.**

STUDY SKILLS

Preparing to study

Devise a study plan

Determine which times of the week you will study.

Split these times into sessions of at least one hour for study of new material. Any shorter periods could be used for revision or practice.

Put the times you plan to study onto a study plan for the weeks from now until the assessment and set yourself targets for each period of study – in your sessions make sure you cover the whole course, activities and the associated questions in the workbook at the back of the manual.

If you are studying more than one unit at a time, try to vary your subjects as this can help to keep you interested and see subjects as part of wider knowledge.

When working through your course, compare your progress with your plan and, if necessary, re-plan your work (perhaps including extra sessions) or, if you are ahead, do some extra revision / practice questions.

Effective studying

Active reading

You are not expected to learn the text by rote, rather, you must understand what you are reading and be able to use it to pass the assessment and develop good practice.

A good technique is to use SQ3Rs – Survey, Question, Read, Recall, Review:

1   **Survey the chapter**

    Look at the headings and read the introduction, knowledge, skills and content, so as to get an overview of what the chapter deals with.

2   **Question**

    Whilst undertaking the survey ask yourself the questions you hope the chapter will answer for you.

3 Read

Read through the chapter thoroughly working through the activities and, at the end, making sure that you can meet the learning objectives highlighted on the first page.

4 Recall

At the end of each section and at the end of the chapter, try to recall the main ideas of the section / chapter without referring to the text. This is best done after short break of a couple of minutes after the reading stage.

5 Review

Check that your recall notes are correct.

You may also find it helpful to re-read the chapter to try and see the topic(s) it deals with as a whole.

Note taking

Taking notes is a useful way of learning, but do not simply copy out the text. The notes must:

- be in your own words
- be concise
- cover the key points
- well organised
- be modified as you study further chapters in this text or in related ones.

Trying to summarise a chapter without referring to the text can be a useful way of determining which areas you know and which you don't.

Three ways of taking notes

1 Summarise the key points of a chapter

2 Make linear notes

A list of headings, subdivided with sub-headings listing the key points.

If you use linear notes, you can use different colours to highlight key points and keep topic areas together.

Use plenty of space to make your notes easy to use.

KAPLAN PUBLISHING

3 Try a diagrammatic form

The most common of which is a mind map.

To make a mind map, put the main heading in the centre of the paper and put a circle around it.]

Draw lines radiating from this to the main sub-headings which again have circles around them.

Continue the process from the sub-headings to sub-sub-headings.

Highlighting and underlining

You may find it useful to underline or highlight key points in your study text – but do be selective.

You may also wish to make notes in the margins.

Revision phase

Kaplan has produced material specifically designed for your final examination preparation for this unit.

These include pocket revision notes and a bank of revision questions specifically in the style of the new syllabus.

Further guidance on how to approach the final stage of your studies is given in these materials.

Further reading

In addition to this text, you should also read the "Student section" of the "Accounting Technician" magazine every month to keep abreast of any guidance from the examiners.

Terminology

There are different terms used to mean the same thing – you will need to be aware of both sets of terminology.

UK GAAP	IAS
Profit and Loss	Income Statement
Sales	Revenue
Balance Sheet	Statement of Financial Position
Fixed Assets	Non-current Assets
Tangible Assets	Property, Plant and Equipment
Stock	Inventory
Trade Debtors	Trade Receivables
Trade Creditors	Trade Payables
Capital	Equity
Profit	Retained Earnings

Cost classification

1

Introduction

This chapter introduces the concepts of financial and management accounting, the terminology of cost, profit and investment centres and looks in detail at different ways of classifying costs.

KNOWLEDGE
Explain the purpose and structure of a costing system within an organisation (1.2)
Describe the relationships between the costing and accounting systems within the organisation (1.3)
Identify materials, labour and expenses and explain how they are classified and recorded (2.1)
Explain fixed variable and semi-variable overheads (2.2)
Identify types of cost and profit centres (2.3)

SKILLS
Distinguish between fixed, variable and semi-variable overheads (1.3)

CONTENTS

1 Financial accounting and management accounting
2 Terminology – cost units and cost centres
3 Cost classification

1 Financial accounting and management accounting

1.1 Introduction

Most businesses, whether large or small, generate large numbers of different types of transaction. To make sense of those transactions, they need to be recorded, summarised and analysed. In all businesses, it is the accounts department that performs these tasks.

From the raw data of the business's transactions, accountants provide **information for a wide range of interested parties**. Each party requires, however, slightly different information, dependent upon their interest in the business.

1.2 Financial accounting

Financial accounting provides information to **external groups**, such as the owners of the business, potential investors and HM Revenue and Customs.

Financial accounting could be described in simple terms as **keeping score**. The financial accounts produced are a **historic record** of transactions and are presented in a standard format laid down in law. These normally include

- A statement of financial position (also known as a balance sheet)
- An income statement (also known as a profit and loss account)

Such statements are normally only produced **once or twice a year**.

Financial accounting is not, however, the only type of accounting. The other main type is management accounting.

1.3 Management accounting

Management accounting provides information for **internal users**, such as the managers of the business.

Management accounting compares **actual results with predicted results** and tries to use information to make further predictions about the future.

It also provides information which managers can use to make **decisions**.

Management accounts can be produced in any format that is useful to the business and tend to be produced frequently, for instance every month.

1.4 The aims of management accounting

The aim of management accounting is to assist management in the following areas of running a business.

- **Planning**

  For example, through the preparation of annual budgets. This is a key aspect of management accounting.

- **Co-ordinating**

  Planning enables all departments to be co-ordinated and to work together.

- **Controlling**

  The comparison of actual results with the budget helps to identify areas where operations are not running according to plan.

  Investigating the causes, and acting on the results of that investigation, helps to control the activities of the business.

- **Communicating**

  Preparing budgets that are distributed to department managers helps to communicate the aims of the business to those managers.

- **Motivating**

  Management accounts include targets. These should motivate managers (and staff) and improve their performance.

  If the target is too difficult, however, it is likely to demotivate and it is unlikely to be achieved.

1.5 Useful management information

For **management information** to be of use to a particular group of managers, it must have the following attributes:

- **Relevant to their responsibilities**. For example, a production manager will want information about stocks, production levels, production performance, etc within his particular department.

- **Relevant to particular decisions**. For example, if deciding whether to close a division, managers would need to know the likely costs including lost sales, likely redundancies and so on.

- **Timely**. Information has to be up-to-date to be of any value.

- **Value**. The benefits of having the information must outweigh the cost of producing it.

1.6 Cost accounting

Cost accounting is part of management accounting. As its name suggests, it is concerned with **establishing costs**. It developed within manufacturing businesses where costs are most difficult to isolate and analyse.

Cost accounting is primarily directed at enabling management to perform the functions of **planning, control** and **decision making:**

(a)   determining costs and profits during a control period

(b)   valuing stocks of raw materials, work in progress and finished goods, and controlling stock levels

(c)   preparing budgets, forecasts and other control data for a forthcoming control period

(d)   creating a reporting system which enables managers to take corrective action where necessary to control costs

(e)   providing information for decision-making such as pricing, for example.

Items (a) and (b) are traditional **cost accounting roles**; (c) to (e) extend into management accounting.

Activity 1

The table below lists some of the characteristics of financial accounting and management accounting systems.

Indicate the characteristics for each system by putting a tick in the relevant column of the table.

Characteristic	Financial Accounting	Management Accounting
Content can include anything useful		
To help managers run the business		
Formats dictated by accounting rules		
Looks mainly at historical information		
Produced for shareholders		

---

2   Terminology – cost units and cost centres

2.1   Cost units

To help with the above purposes of planning, control and decision making, businesses often need to calculate a cost per unit of output.

A key question, however, is what exactly we mean by a "unit of output", or "**cost unit**". This will mean different things to different businesses but we always looks at what the business produces.

- A car manufacturer will want to determine the cost of each car and probably different components as well.

- In a printing firm, the cost unit could be the specific customer order.

- For a paint manufacturer, the unit could be a litre of paint.

- An accountancy firm will want to know the costs incurred for each client. To help with this it is common to calculate the cost per hour of chargeable time spent by staff.

- A hospital might wish to calculate the cost per patient treated, the cost of providing a bed for each day or the cost of an operation, say.

2.2   Cost centres

A **cost centre** is a small part of a business for which costs are determined. This varies from business to business but could include any of the following:

- The Research and Development department

- The Human Resources function

- A warehouse

- A factory in a particular location

It is important to recognise that cost centre costs are necessary for control purposes, as well as for relating costs to cost units. This is because the manager of a cost centre will be responsible for the costs incurred.

Activity 2

Suggest **ONE** suitable cost unit and **TWO** cost centres for a college of further education.

2.3 Cost, profit and investment centres

Some businesses use the term "cost centre" in a more precise way than that given above:

- A **cost centre** is when the manager of the centre (department or division or location or...) is responsible for costs but not revenue or investment. This is usually because the centre has no revenue stream.

  For example, a research and development department.

- A **profit centre** is when the manager of the centre (department or division or location or...) is responsible for costs and revenues but not investment.

  For example, a local supermarket where investment decisions are made by the main Board.

- An **investment centre** is when the manager of the centre (usually a division) is responsible for costs and revenues **and** the level of investment in the division.

  For example, the US subsidiary of a global firm. The CEO would usually have authority to open new factories, close others and so on.

3 Cost classification

3.1 Types of cost classification

Costs can be **classified** (collected into logical groups) in many ways. The particular classification selected will depend upon the purpose for which the resulting analysed data will be used, for example:

Purpose	Classification
Financial accounts	By function - Cost of sales, distribution costs, administrative expenses.
Cost control	By element – materials, labour, other expenses
Cost accounts	By relationship to cost units – direct, indirect
Budgeting, decision making	By behaviour – fixed, variable

3.2   Cost classification by function

For financial accounting purposes costs are split into the following categories:

- **Cost of sales** – also known as production costs. This category could include production labour, materials, supervisor salaries and factory rent.

- **Distribution costs** – this includes selling and distribution costs such as sales team commission and delivery costs.

- **Administrative costs** – this includes head office costs, IT support, HR support and so on.

Note that one cost you will meet in the exam is depreciation. This is a measure of how much an asset is wearing out or being used up. The classification will depend on which asset is being depreciated. For example,

- Cost of sales – depreciation on a machine in the production line

- Distribution – depreciation of a delivery van

- Admin – depreciation of a computer in the accounts department

---

Activity 3

James plc makes mobile phones. Classify the following costs by function in the table below.

Cost	Production	Admin.	Distribution
Purchases of plastic to make phone cases			
IT director's bonus			
Depreciation of factory building			
Salaries of production workers			
Insurance of sales team laptops			

3.3   Cost classification by element

The simplest classification you will meet in the exam is splitting costs according to element as follows:

- **Materials -** includes raw materials for a manufacturer or alternatively the cost of goods that are to be resold in a retail organisation

- **Labour -** Labour costs can consist of not only basic pay but overtime, commissions and bonuses as well.

- **Other expenses** – this includes electricity, depreciation, rent and so on.

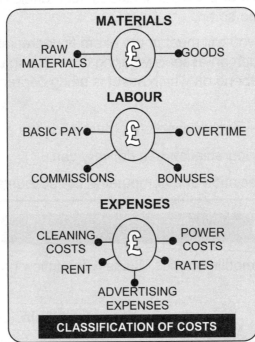

CLASSIFICATION OF COSTS

Activity 4

Classify the following costs for a supermarket chain by element in the table below.

Cost	Materials	Labour	Expenses
Tins of baked beans			
Lighting costs			
Depreciation of freezers			
Checkout staff salaries			
Flour used in in-store bakery			

3.4   Cost classification by nature – direct and indirect

To make calculating a cost per unit easier costs are split into the following categories:

- A **direct** cost is an item of cost that is traceable directly to a cost unit.

  For example, the cost of a bought-in lights for a car manufacturer.

  The total of all direct costs is known as the "prime cost" per unit.

  An **indirect** cost is a cost that either cannot easily be identified with any one finished unit. Such costs are often referred to as "overheads".

  For example, the rent on a factory.

Activity 5

Chadwicks runs a car repair service and garage. Classify the following costs by nature (direct or indirect) in the table below.

Cost	Direct	Indirect
Engine oil used in services		
Receptionist's wages		
Annual repairs to engine crane		
Brake pads		

Activity 6

JJ Green is a furniture manufacturer. Classify the following costs by nature (direct or indirect) in the table below.

Cost	Direct	Indirect
Cost of wood and screws used		
Royalty payable as a result of using a particular chair design		
Oil used to lubricate the machines		
Salesmen's salaries		

3.5   Cost classification by behaviour – fixed and variable

For budgeting purposes, management needs to be able to predict **how costs will vary with differing levels of activity** (i.e. the number of cost units).

For example, if a furniture manufacturer expected to produce 1,000 chairs in a particular month, what should he budget for the costs of wood, labour, oil, selling costs, factory heat and light, manager's salaries, etc? How would these costs differ (if at all) if he expected to produce 2,000 chairs?

To make budgeting and forecasting easier, costs are split into the following categories:

- **Variable costs** are those that vary (usually assumed in direct proportion) with changes in level of activity

    For example, if you make twice the number of chairs then the amount (and hence the cost) of wood used would double.

- **Fixed costs** are not affected by changes in activity level.

    For example, the rent on the factory.

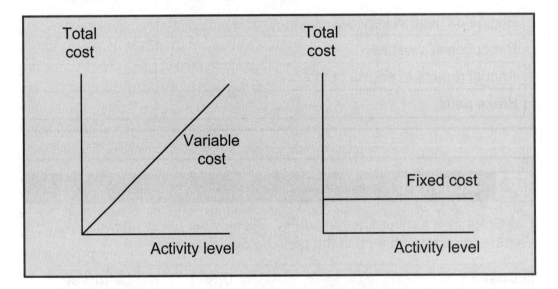

- **Semi-variable costs** are those that have a fixed element and a variable element.

    For example, the cost of electricity for the factory has a fixed element relating to lighting and a variable element relating to power used on the production line.

    KAPLAN PUBLISHING

- **Stepped costs** are costs that remain fixed up to a particular level of activity, but which rise to a higher (fixed) level if activity goes beyond that range.

   For example, a firm may pay £40,000 per year to rent a factory in which they can produce up to 1 million units of product per year. However, if demand increases to more than 1 million units a second factory may be required, in which case the cost of factory rent may step up to, say, £80,000 per year and then be constant until we want to make 3 million.

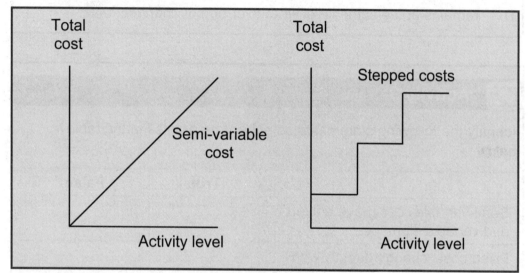

Activity 7

The Grande is a hotel in Wales. Classify the following costs by their behaviour in the table below.

Cost	Fixed	Variable	Semi-variable
Manager's salary			
Cleaning materials			
Food served in the restaurant			
Electricity – includes a standing charge			
Cleaner's wages (paid per room cleaned)			

Activity 8

Which of the following best describes a 'pure' fixed cost?

A cost which:

A   represents a fixed proportion of total costs

B   remains at the same level up to a particular level of output

C   has a direct relationship with output

D   remains at the same level whenever output changes.

Activity 9

Identify the following statements as either true or false in the table below.

	True	False
Semi-variable costs have a fixed and variable element		
Fixed costs change directly with changes in activity		
Variable costs change directly with changes in activity		

3.6   Combining cost classifications

In some tasks in your assessment you may have to use more than one classification at a time. For example,

- Factory rent is a production cost that is fixed (or stepped) and indirect.

- Direct materials are a production cost that is also variable

- Direct labour is not necessarily a variable cost. For a car repair service, for example, it is possible to identify how much time a particular repair takes (by using job cards to record time) but the mechanic may be on a fixed salary per month.

- Sales commission is a variable selling and distribution cost.

Activity 10

Identify the following statements as either true or false in the table below.

	True	False
All direct costs are variable		
All overheads are fixed		
Depreciation is always classified as an administrative cost		
All selling costs are fixed		

4 Summary

In this introductory chapter we looked at some of the basic principles and terminology used in cost and management accounting. Costs can be classified in a variety of different ways for different purposes.

The basic classification is into materials, labour and expenses, each of which will be dealt with in detail in the following chapters.

A further method of classification of costs is between direct and indirect costs. You need to be aware of the difference between cost units (individual units of a product or service for which costs can be separately ascertained) and cost centres (locations or functions in respect of which costs are accumulated).

For decision-making and budgeting purposes, it is often useful to distinguish costs according to their behaviour as production levels change. The basic classifications according to behaviour are fixed and variable costs although there are also stepped costs and semi-variable costs.

Answers to chapter activities

Activity 1

Characteristic	Financial Accounting	Management Accounting
Content can include anything useful		☑
To help managers run the business		☑
Formats dictated by accounting rules	☑	
Looks mainly at historical information	☑	
Produced for shareholders	☑	

Activity 2

Student hours	=	Cost unit
Computer room and library	=	Cost centres

Activity 3

Cost	Production	Admin.	Distribution
Purchases of plastic to make phone cases	☑		
IT director's bonus		☑	
Depreciation of factory building	☑		
Salaries of production workers	☑		
Insurance of sales team laptops			☑

KAPLAN PUBLISHING

Activity 4

Cost	Materials	Labour	Expenses
Tins of baked beans	☑		
Lighting costs			☑
Depreciation of freezers			☑
Checkout staff salaries		☑	
Flour used in in-store bakery	☑		

Activity 5

Cost	Direct	Indirect
Engine oil used in services	☑	
Receptionist's wages		☑
Annual repairs to engine crane		☑
Brake pads	☑	

Activity 6

Cost	Direct	Indirect
Cost of wood and screws used	☑	
Royalty payable as a result of using a particular chair design	☑	
Oil used to lubricate the machines		☑
Salesmen's salaries		☑

Note: You may have argued that oil was direct as you could calculate how much oil is needed per item made. However, it would be very difficult to determine the oil need for a **particular** item of furniture; hence the correct answer is indirect.

Activity 7

Cost	Fixed	Variable	Semi-variable
Manager's salary	☑		
Cleaning materials		☑	
Food in restaurant		☑	
Electricity – includes a standing charge			☑
Cleaner's wages (paid per room cleaned)		☑	

Activity 8

D – Pure fixed costs remain exactly the same in total regardless of the activity level.

Activity 9

	True	False
Semi-variable costs have a fixed and variable element	☑	
Fixed costs change directly with changes in activity		☑
Variable costs change directly with changes in activity	☑	

Activity 10

	True	False
All direct costs are variable		☑ Note 1
All overheads are fixed		☑ Note 2
Depreciation is always classified as an administrative cost		☑ Note 3
All selling costs are fixed		☑ Note 4

Note 1: Whereas direct materials are usually variable, direct labour may be fixed – e.g. lawyers may be on a fixed salary but produce detailed timesheets so a direct labour cost can be calculated for each client.

Note 2: Electricity is usually classified as an overhead but will have a variable element. If more units are made on a production line, then more electricity will be used (hence variable). However, it may not be possible or practical to measure exactly how much electricity is used to make a particular unit (hence indirect).

Note 3: For example, depreciation on production machinery would be included in cost of sales.

Note 4: Sales commission would be a variable selling cost.

5   Test your knowledge

Workbook Activity 11

The table below lists some of the characteristics of financial accounting and management accounting systems. Indicate the characteristics for each system by putting a tick in the relevant column of the table.

Characteristic	Financial Accounting	Management Accounting
Content can include forecasts		
Looks mainly at historical information		
Format must conform to statute and accounting standards		
Any format can be used		
Mainly produced to help managers run and control the business		
Would be used by potential investors thinking of buying shares		
Produced for shareholders		

KAPLAN PUBLISHING

Workbook Activity 12

Zenawi plc makes garden furniture.

Classify the following costs by function in the table below.

Cost	Production	Admin.	Distribution
Purchases of wood to make chairs			
Depreciation of delivery vans			
HR director's bonus			
Salaries of production workers			
Electricity bill for workshop			
Insurance of sales team laptops			

Workbook Activity 13

Kim and Yoshiro are the founding partners of an accountancy firm. They employ 20 accountants and have over 100 clients.

Classify the following costs by nature (direct or indirect) in the table below.

Cost	Direct	Indirect
Travelling costs for when staff visit clients		
Rechargeable accountants' time		
Office heating costs		
Recruitment costs		
Accountants' time recorded as "general admin." on time sheets		

Workbook Activity 14

Elite Cars is a family-run business specialising in the sale, hire, servicing and repair of classic cars.

Classify the following costs by their behaviour in the table below.

Cost	Fixed	Variable	Semi-variable
Sales staff pay			
Motor oil used in servicing			
Depreciation of premises			
Mechanics' pay (salaried)			
Electricity			

Coding of costs and income

2

Introduction

This chapter looks at the use of coding in organisations, including how income and expenditure is coded.

KNOWLEDGE
Identify materials, labour and expenses and explain how they are classified and recorded (2.1)

SKILLS
Explain different methods of coding data (2.4)

CONTENTS

1   Classification and coding of costs
2   Coding in practice
3   Problems with coding

1 Classification and coding of costs

Cost accountants need to determine the costs that relate to each cost or profit centre. To make this simpler, each expense is classified according to its cost centre and type of expense.

A cost code is then allocated to the expense to represent this classification.

1.1 Coding systems

> **Definition**
>
> A **code** is a system of symbols designed to be applied to a classified set of items, to give a brief, accurate reference, which helps entry to the records, collation and analysis.

A cost code is a code used in a costing system.

1.2 Cost codes

In general, cost codes are constructed by deciding on the information that is needed. For most businesses we want to identify

(a)   the profit or cost centre that is incurring the cost and

(b)   the type of cost that is incurred.

There are no set methods of designing a cost code and the cost code of a particular organisation will be that which best suits the operations and costs of that business.

For example, if a business has only one division/operating centre, then there will be no need to identify that centre in the cost code. But if a business has several divisions, then the division that incurs the cost will need to be identified in the cost code.

Similarly, if the divisions have several cost centres and incur several different types of cost, then the cost code must be able to identify each of these.

Example

Consider a company that has two operating divisions (North and South), two cost centres in each division (construction and despatch) with each cost centre incurring three types of cost (material, labour and expenses)

A typical cost code could be devised as follows

Step 1 Decide the structure of the cost code, for example **/**/**, where

First two digits	the operating division
Second two digits	the cost centre
Third two digits	the type of cost

Step 2 Allocate code numbers to the elements

(a) two operating divisions

North	01
South	02

(b) each division has two cost centres

Construction	01
Despatch	02

(c) each cost centre incurs three types of cost

Materials	01
Labour	02
Expense	03

Examples

Thus a cost code for expenses incurred by the despatch centre of the North division would be:

First two digits	the operating division	North	01
Second two digits	the cost centre	despatch	02
Third two digits	the type of cost	expenses	03

The cost code would therefore be: 01/02/03

Similarly, the code for materials purchased by the construction centre of the South would be 02/01/01.

1.3   More complex codes

Once a cost has been allocated its correct cost centre code then it may also be useful to know the particular type of expense involved. Therefore some more digits might be added to the cost centre code to represent the precise type of cost.

Example

If an expense for Machine Group 7 is for oil then its code might be 07 (for its cost centre) followed by 23 to represent materials followed by 04 to represent oil.

If an expense of the canteen is identified as frozen peas then its cost code might be 16 (its cost centre) followed by 02 to represent food purchases (materials) followed by 19 to represent frozen peas.

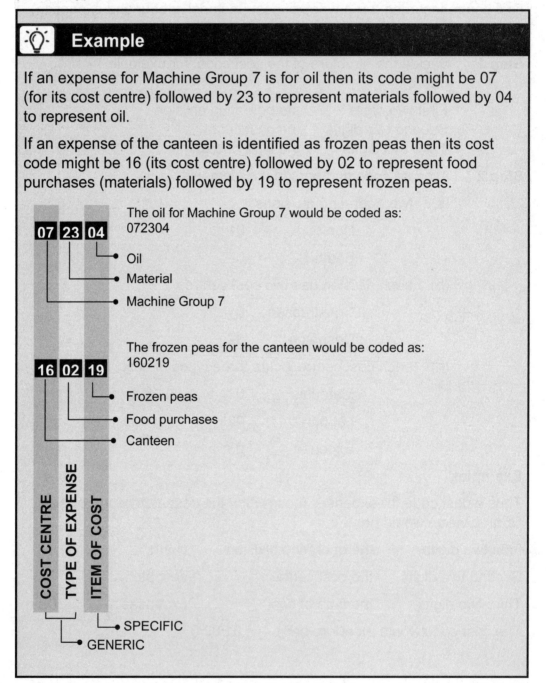

Activity 1

Greggs Ltd, a manufacturer of garden lighting, uses a numerical coding structure based on one profit centre and three cost centres as outlined below. Each code has a sub-code so each transaction will be coded as ***/***.

Profit / cost centre	Code	Sub-classification	Sub-code
Sales	100	Sales to the public	100
		Sales to retailers	200
Production	200	Direct costs	100
		Indirect costs	200
Selling and distribution	300	Direct costs	100
		Indirect costs	200
Administration	400	Direct costs	100
		Indirect costs	200

Code the following revenue and expense transactions, which have been extracted from purchase invoices, sales invoices and payroll, using the table below.

Transaction	Code
Wages for staff working in the factory canteen	
Sales to a French retailer	
Sales to individuals via the company website	
Depreciation on cars provided to salesmen	
Bulbs for use in the garden lighting products	
Chief accountant's salary	

Activity 2

Owen Ltd manufactures motorbike helmets.

It has two factories that are coded as:

Slough	S
Leeds	L

Each factory has the following cost centres:

Machining	120
Finishing	121
Packing	122
Stores	123
Canteen	124
Maintenance	125
Administration	126

Type of expense:

Labour	200
Material	201
Expenses	202

Sales revenue:	210

Thus, the cost of production labour in the Finishing Department at the Leeds factory would be coded L/121/200.

Code the following expenses using the table below.

Transaction	Code
Slough factory, cleaning materials used in the canteen	
Slough factory, wages for stores personnel	
Leeds factory, electricity for Machining Department	
Leeds factory, telephone account for site as a whole	
Slough factory, general maintenance material for repairs.	

1.4 Types of code

There are a number of different methods of coding data:

- **numeric:** e.g. 100/310

- **alphabetic**: e.g. AB/RT

- **alpha-numeric**: e.g. A230

1.5 Purpose of cost codes

The main purposes of cost codes are to:

- **assist precise information:** costs incurred can be associated with pre-established codes, so reducing variations in classification

- **facilitate electronic data processing:** computer analysis, summarisation and presentation of data can be performed more easily through the use of codes

- **facilitate a logical and systematic arrangement of costing records:** accounts can be arranged in blocks of codes permitting additional codes to be inserted in logical order

- **simplify comparison of totals of similar expenses** rather than all of the individual items

- **incorporate check codes** within the main code to check the accuracy of the postings.

 Coding in practice

2.1 Timing of coding

In order to be of most use the coding of costs should take place when the cost or expense is first received by the organisation. In most cases this will be when the invoice for the goods is received.

After this point the documents will be entered into the accounting system and then to the filing system so it is important that the coding is done immediately.

2.2 Receiving an invoice

When an invoice is received by the organisation it will undergo a variety of checks to ensure that it is for valid purchases that were ordered and have been received or that it is for a service that has been received.

In the process of these checks it will become clear what type of goods or service is being dealt with, for example it may be an invoice for the purchase of raw materials for the factory or an electricity bill for the entire organisation.

Once the invoice has been checked for validity then it must be correctly coded.

2.3 Choosing the correct code

In order for the correct code to be given to the invoice, it is vital that the person responsible for the coding fully understands the nature of the organisation and the costs that it incurs. The organisation's coding listing should be referred to and the correct cost centre, type and expense code should be entered on the front of the invoice.

2.4 Cheque and cash payments

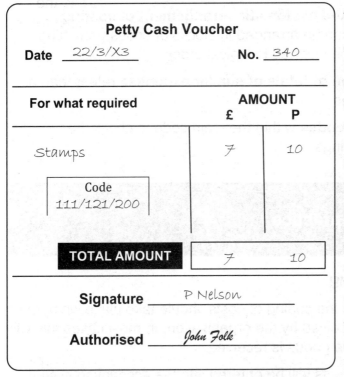

As well as receiving invoices for costs incurred on credit most organisations will also write cheques for costs and even pay some costs out of petty cash. These costs must be coded in just the same way as purchases or expenses on credit.

If the payment is by cheque then there will be some documentation to support that payment. When this documentation is authorised for payment then it should also be coded for costing purposes.

If payments are made out of petty cash then they must be supported by a petty cash voucher. Again this voucher must be coded according to the type of cost.

2.5 Shared costs

Shared costs are costs that do not relate specifically to a particular cost centre. Some costs, for example electricity bills, cannot be allocated directly to a single cost centre as they are indirect costs which relate to a number of cost centres. Eventually a portion of this electricity bill will be shared out to each of the cost centres that uses electricity but at the point where the account is being coded it must simply be recognised that this is a shared cost and not a cost that should be coded to a particular cost centre.

Therefore, the coding structure of the organisation should include some codes that specifically identify a cost as a shared cost.

2.6   Payment of wages and salaries

Wages and salaries normally form a very large part of the costs incurred by an organisation. If wages or salaries are paid by cheque or in cash then the supporting documentation, the payslip, should be coded as with other cash payments.

However frequently wages and salaries will usually be paid directly into employee's bank accounts through the BACS system. Therefore it is important that the wages and salaries costs are coded according to the department or cost centre so that the total labour cost of the cost centre is known.

2.7   Sales invoices

If an organisation makes sales on credit then when the sales invoice is produced it should be coded according to the coding listing.

This code will probably specify the profit centre or investment centre that has made the sale and often also the product that is being sold.

2.8   Cash sales

In a retail organisation sales may be made for cash.

There should always be documentation that supports the cash takings, such as the till rolls for the day. This documentation then needs to be coded to reflect the profit or investment centre that made the sales and any other detailed product coding that is required by the organisation.

Most modern cash registers will automatically record and code each sale using the bar code on the product.

2.9   Assets and liabilities

We have concentrated so far on the costing of costs and revenue. However there are other items that also need to be coded, for example assets and liabilities.

The sort of assets that may occur in the exam are fixed assets (or "non-current assets") purchased for the business and current assets (for example, debtors or "receivables").

 Example

Codebreaker Ltd manufactures the Enigma game machine.

The company has bought a production machine for £5,000.

The coding system is structured as:

- First two digits refer to the profit centre (the Enigma machine is profit centre 08).

- The additional code digits for fixed assets for production are 2600.

The code for the expenditure made by purchasing the machine are

    £5,000   082600

These codes would be the instruction to the accountant (or the computer) to post £5,000 to the appropriate fixed asset account.

---

3 Problems with coding

3.1 Which code?

The main problem when coding documents is deciding which cost centre and analysis code to use; the documents may not clearly show which cost centre incurred the costs or the type of cost it is.

If you are unable to code a document try:

- looking in the organisation's procedures manual

- referring the query document to your supervisor.

3.2 Apportionment

As mentioned above, if more than one cost centre has incurred the cost (for example, a heating bill for the whole building), the cost needs to be shared between all of the cost centres (or apportioned).

Although it may be easy to simply share the costs equally between the cost centres, some cost centres may be bigger than others and therefore use more electricity/heating etc – so should receive a greater percentage of the cost.

You will learn more about methods of cost apportionment in the level 3 unit "Costs and Revenues".

Summary

You should now know the importance of coding of costs and income. If actual costs and income are to be used for management purposes then it is vital that they are correctly classified and coded to ensure that they are allocated to the correct cost, profit or investment centre and according to the correct type of costs - material, labour or expense. Only then can any useful management information be obtained.

Answers to chapter activities

Activity 1

Transaction	Code
Wages for staff working in the factory canteen	200/200
Sales to a French retailer	100/200
Sales to individuals via the company website	100/100
Depreciation on cars provided to salesmen	300/200
Bulbs for use in the garden lighting products	200/100
Chief accountant's salary	400/200

Activity 2

Transaction	Code
Slough factory, cleaning materials used in the canteen	S/124/201
Slough factory, wages for stores personnel	S/123/200
Leeds factory, electricity for Machining Department	L/120/202
Leeds factory, telephone account for site as a whole	L/126/202
Slough factory, general maintenance material for repairs.	S/125/201

5 Test your knowledge

Workbook Activity 3

A company manufactures shoes and slippers in half-sizes in the following size ranges:

- Men's 6 to 9½
- Ladies 3 to 9
- Boys 1 to 5½
- Girls 1 to 5

The company uses a seven-digit code to identify its finished products, which, reading from left to right, is built up as follows:

Digit one indicates whether the products are mens, ladies, boys or girls. The numbers used are

1	–	mens
2	–	ladies
3	–	boys
4	–	girls

Digit two denotes type of footwear (3 is shoes; 6 is slippers)

Digit three denotes colour (5 is green; 6 is burgundy)

Digit four denotes the material of the upper part of the product (leather is 4)

Digit five denotes the material of the sole (leather is 1)

Digits six and seven denote size.

Example

(i)   Code 1613275 represents a pair of Men's slippers, brown suede, rubber sole, size 7½

Task: Set suitable code numbers to the following:

Product	Code
Boys' shoes, brown leather uppers, rubber soles, size 4	
Ladies' slippers, green suede uppers, rubber soles, size 4½	
Girls' shoes, burgundy leather uppers, leather soles, size 3½.	

Workbook Activity 4

The expenses of an international organisation are coded with a seven digit code system as follows:

First and second digits   –   location
Third and fourth digits   –   function
Final three digits   –   type of expense

Extracts from within the costing system are as follows:

Location	Code	Function	Code
London	10	Production	20
Dublin	11	Marketing	21
Lagos	12	Accounts	23
Nairobi	13	Administration	24
Kuala Lumpur	17		
Hong Kong	18	**Type of expense**	**Code**
		Factory rent	201
		Stationery	202
		Telephone	203
		Travel	204
		Entertainment	205

Examples of the codes are as follows:

Factory rent in Nairobi: 1320201
Stationery purchased in London office: 1024202

Task

Code the following revenue and expense transactions, which have been extracted from purchase invoices, sales invoices and payroll, using the table below.

Transaction	Code
Factory rent in the Dublin factory.	
Administration telephone costs incurred in Lagos.	
Salesman in Hong Kong entertaining an overseas visitor	
Marketing brochures ordered in London	

     KAPLAN PUBLISHING

BASIC COSTING

Materials and stock

3

Introduction

This chapter considers in more detail materials, the different types of stock and how stocks are valued and classified.

KNOWLEDGE
Identify materials, labour and expenses and explain how they are classified and recorded (2.1)
Identify different types of stock (2.5)
• Raw materials
• Part-finished goods (work in progress)
• Finished goods
Explain different methods of stock valuation (2.6)

SKILLS
Calculate stock valuations using different methods (1.5)

CONTENTS

1 Different types of stock
2 Valuing raw materials
3 Valuing WIP and finished goods
4 The materials purchasing cycle in practise

KAPLAN PUBLISHING

35

1 Different types of stock

1.1 The production cycle

For a retailer the main type of stock will be goods bought for resale.

For a manufacturer, however, we can identify three types of stock:

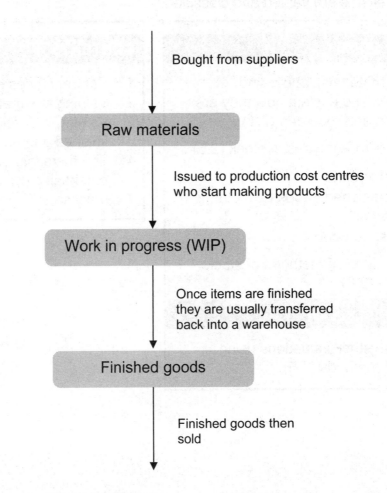

You may also see "stock" referred to as "inventory".

1.2 Materials

For manufacturers various materials are needed to make the main product of the business.

Remember that, for management accounting purposes, costs can be classified as either direct or indirect. Materials are no exception to this.

> ## Definition
>
> **Direct** materials are the materials that are used directly as part of the production of the goods that the organisation makes.

The direct materials are therefore the raw materials that are part of the manufacturing process. In a business that makes wooden furniture the direct materials would for example include wood, hinges and polish.

> ## Definition
>
> **Indirect** materials are other materials used in the production process which are not used in the actual products themselves.

So for example lubricant for the machines that make the wooden furniture would be classified as indirect materials as it would be extremely difficult to identify how much lubricant was used to make a particular chair, say.

1.3 Work in progress

Work in progress (WIP) refers to units that have been started but are incomplete at the end of the accounting period.

For example a wooden table may have had the top made but is still waiting for legs to be attached.

1.4 Finished goods

Finished goods are completed and ready for selling to customers.

2 Valuing raw materials

2.1 Introduction

There are two aspects to valuing raw materials:

- Firstly we need to determine the cost of materials issued to production cost centres.

- Secondly we need to be able to value the stock of raw materials left in stores.

The cost of materials purchased will normally be derived from suppliers' invoices but, where many purchases have been made at differing prices, a decision has to be taken as to which cost is used when stock is issued to the user department (cost centre).

⌾ Example 1

Petra Ltd has the following movements in a certain type of stock into and out of it stores for the month of May:

Date	Receipts			Issues	
	Kg	Price / kg	Cost	Kg	Cost
May 1	200	£9.00	£1,800		
May 2	100	£10.80	£1,080		
May 3				50	?

What is the cost of materials issued on May 3?

Should we use £9/kg, £10.80/kg or something in between?

2.2 Methods of pricing issues of materials

Various methods exist including:

(a) FIFO (first in, first out)

(b) LIFO (last in, first out)

(c) Weighed average (AVCO)

The choice of method will not only affect the charge to the user department for which the material is required, but also the value of the stock left in stores.

These systems attempt to reflect the movements of individual units in and out of stock under different assumptions.

- **FIFO** – assumes that issues will be made from the oldest stock available, leaving the latest purchases in stock. This means that transfers from stores to production will be made at the oldest prices and the newest prices will be used to value the remaining stock.

  FIFO is particularly useful when products are perishable and you want the oldest used first to avoid it going off or becoming out of date e.g. milk .

- **LIFO** – assumes that issues will be made from the newest stock available, leaving the earliest purchases in stock. This means that transfers from stores to production will be made at the newest prices and the older prices will be used to value the remaining stock.

  LIFO could be used when products are not perishable e.g. stationery

- **AVCO** – assumes that the issues into production will be made at an average price. This is calculated by taking the total value of the stock and dividing it by the total units in stock, thus finding the average price per unit. A new average cost is calculated before each issue to production.

  AVCO could be used when individual units of material are not separately definable e.g. sand at a builders merchants.

Example 1 – continued

Petra Ltd has the following movements in a certain type of stock into and out of it stores for the month of May:

Date	Receipts			Issues	
	Kg	Price / kg	Cost	Kg	Cost
May 1	200	£9.00	£1,800		
May 2	100	£10.80	£1,080		
May 3				50	

Complete the table below for the issue and closing stock values.

Method	Cost of issue	Closing stock
FIFO		
LIFO		
AVCO		

Solution

Method	Cost of issue	Closing stock
FIFO	£450	£2,430
LIFO	£540	£2,340
AVCO	£480	£2,400

Workings

FIFO

- The 50kg issued on the 3rd May will all come from the **earliest** purchase made on the 1st May.

- Thus the cost of the issue will be 50kg@9 = £450

- There are two ways to get closing stock.

- The first is to look at the flow of units : closing stock will be 150kg @ £9 (the remaining stock from the 1st May purchase) and 100kg @ £10.80 = £2,430

- The second approach, which will probably be easier in the exam, is to consider total purchases and simply deduct issues. Total purchases = £2,880, so closing stock = 2,880 – 450 = £2,430

LIFO

- The 50kg issued on the 3rd May will all come from the **most recent** purchase made on the 2nd May.

- Thus the cost of the issue will be 50kg@10.80 = £540

- Closing stock = 2,880 – 540 = £2,340

- **OR** closing stock will be 200kg @ £9 (1st May purchase) and 50kg @ £10.80 (the remaining stock from the 2nd May) = £2,340

AVCO

- We bought 300kg at a total cost of 200@9 + 100@10.80 = £2,880

- On average this works out at 2,880/300 = £9.60/kg

- Thus the cost of the issue will be 50kg@9.60 = £480

- Closing stock = 2,880 – 480 = £2,400

- **OR** closing stock carried forwards will have the same average cost per unit so will be 250kg @ £9.60 = £2,400

Activity 1

Krully Ltd has the following movements in a certain type of stock into and out of it stores for the month of June:

Date	Receipts		Issues	
	Units	Cost	Units	Cost
June 2	100	£400		
June 3	200	£1,000		
June 6	200	£1,200		
June 19			400	
June 25	400	£2,500		

Complete the table below for the issue and closing stock values.

Method	Cost of issue on 19 June	Closing stock at 30 June
FIFO	1600	~~1050~~ 3500
LIFO	2400	200 2700
AVCO		

2.3 Features of the different methods

FIFO is fairly easy to understand and has the following features:

- In times of rapidly increasing prices, material may be issued at an early and hence unrealistically low price, resulting in the particular job showing an unusually large profit.

- Two jobs started on the same day may show a different cost for the same quantity of the same material.

- In times of rapidly increasing prices FIFO will give a higher profit figure than LIFO or AVCO.

LIFO is also fairly simple to follow and has the following features:

- In contrast to FIFO closing stocks will now be shown at the earliest prices which means that in times of rapidly increasing or decreasing prices, the stock figure bears little resemblance to the current cost of replacement.

- As with FIFO, two jobs started on the same day may show a different cost for the same quantity of the same material.

- The LIFO method uses the latest prices for issues to production and therefore the cost obtained is more likely to be in line with other costs and selling prices.

- In times of rapidly increasing prices LIFO will give a lower profit figure than FIFO and AVCO.

AVCO is a compromise on valuation of stock and issues and the average price rarely reflects the actual purchase price of the material.

Activity 2

Identify the correct stock valuation method from the characteristic given by putting a tick in the relevant column of the table below.

Characteristic	FIFO	LIFO	AVCO
• Issues are valued at the most recent purchase cost			
• Stock is valued at the average of the cost of purchases			
• Stock is valued at the most recent purchase cost			

Activity 3

Identify the following statements as either true or false.

Statement	True	False
• FIFO costs issues of stock at the most recent purchase price		
• AVCO costs issues of stock at the oldest purchase price		
• LIFO costs issues of stock at the oldest purchase price		
• FIFO values closing stock at the most recent purchase price		
• LIFO values closing stock at the most recent purchase price		
• AVCO values closing stock at the latest purchase price		

3 Valuing WIP and finished goods

3.1 Basic principles

When valuing WIP or finished goods we need to incorporate all the different costs incurred to bring it to its present location and condition. To make this easier, direct costs are included first and then indirect costs or overheads added.

Identifying direct materials and labour should be straightforward, or the costs would not be classified as "direct":

- Direct materials could be identified using job cards and information on stores requisitions.

- Direct labour can be identified using job cards and time sheets.

Because it is more difficult to identify overheads with units of output some system needs to be developed for either averaging overheads over units or absorbing them into units. This is particularly important when a company makes more than one product.

This is discussed in more detail in the "Costs and Revenues" unit but here you need to be aware of two approaches:

- Unit basis - each unit gets the same level of overhead.

- Labour rate basis - here overheads are absorbed as a rate per direct labour hour. This means that for every hour someone works on the unit an hour's worth of overhead is given to the unit as well.

Example 2

The cost per unit for completed goods could show the following:

	Cost/unit £
Direct labour cost (2 hours @£10/hour)	20
Direct material cost	3
Direct expenses	1
Prime cost	24
Production overheads (2 hours @ £4/hour)	8
Total cost per unit	32

Example 3

A job card showing the WIP on job number 217 might look like the following:

JOB NO	217		
Materials requisitions	**Quantity**	**£**	**Total**
0254 G 3578	100 kg	4,200	
0261 K 3512	50 kg	3,150	
		———	7,350
Wages – employees	**Hours**	**£**	
13343	80	656	
15651	30	300	
12965	40	360	
	———	———	
	150		1,316
	———		
Overheads	**Hours**	**£**	
Absorption rate £12	150	1,800	1,800
		———	
Total cost			10,466
			———

3.2 Calculating a cost per unit

In the exam you may be asked to calculate a unit cost at a specified production level. When doing this, be careful to distinguish between fixed and variable costs and do not confuse total costs and unit costs.

Example 4

Baker Ltd is costing a single product which has the following cost details

Variable Costs per unit

Materials	£5
Labour	£6
Total Fixed Costs	£70,000

Complete the following total cost and unit cost table for a production level of 20,000 units.

Element	Total Cost	Unit cost
Materials	£	£
Labour	£	£
Overheads	£	£
Total	£	£

Solution

Element	Total Cost	Unit cost
Materials	£100,000	£5.00
Labour	£120,000	£6.00
Overheads	£70,000	£3.50
Total	£290,000	£14.50

Workings

Materials:

- This is a variable cost - unit cost is £5 (given)
- Total cost will be 20,000×5 = £100,000

Labour:

- This is a variable cost - unit cost is £6 (given)
- Total cost will be 20,000×6 = £120,000

Overheads

- This is a fixed cost - total cost is £70,000 (given)
- Unit cost will be 70,000÷20,000 = £3.50

Activity 4

XYZ Ltd is costing a single product which has the following cost details

Variable Costs per unit

Materials	£4
Labour	£5
Total Fixed Costs	£60,000

Complete the following total cost and unit cost table for a production level of 15,000 units.

Element	Total Cost	Unit cost
Materials	£	£
Labour	£	£
Overheads	£	£
Total	£	£

Example 5

Complete the table below showing fixed costs, variable costs, total costs and unit cost at the different levels of production.

Units	Fixed Costs	Variable Costs	Total Costs	Unit Cost
1,000	£20,000	£4,000	£24,000	£24.00
2,000	£	£	£	£
3,000	£	£	£	£
4,000	£	£	£	£

Solution

Units	Fixed Costs	Variable Costs	Total Costs	Unit Cost
1,000	£20,000	£4,000	£24,000	£24.00
2,000	£20,000	£8,000	£28,000	£14.00
3,000	£20,000	£12,000	£32,000	£10.67
4,000	£20,000	£16,000	£36,000	£9.00

Workings

Fixed costs:

- Unless there are stepped costs, the fixed costs will be the same at each activity level

Variable costs – approach 1

- Calculate the variable cost per unit = £4,000/1,000 units = £4 per unit.

- This can then be used to get the total variable cost at different levels.

- So for 3,000 units the total variable cost will be 3,000 × 4 = £12,000

Variable costs – approach 2

- Alternatively you could scale up the total variable cost.

- For example, going from 1,000 to 3,000 units we have increased the number of units by a factor of 3 so need to do the same to the variable costs.

- This gives total variable cost = 3 × 4,000 = £12,000 as before.

Unit costs

- Simply divide the total cost by the number of units

- E.g. for 4,000 units, unit costs = £36,000 / 4,000 = £9 per unit

---

Activity 5

Complete the table below showing fixed costs, variable costs, total costs and unit cost at the different levels of production.

Units	Fixed Costs	Variable Costs	Total Costs	Unit Cost
1,000	£60,000	£2,000	£62,000	£62.00
2,000	£	£	£	£
3,000	£	£	£	£
4,000	£	£	£	£

3.3 Factory cost of goods sold

As well as valuing units for stock purposes we also want to know the cost of goods sold. The main issue here is that we need to adjust the costs incurred within the period to take into account opening and closing stock.

For a retailer:

Cost of sales = opening stock + purchases – closing stock

For a manufacturer there will be the further complication that there will be opening and closing stocks for raw materials, work in progress and finished goods. This could be shown as a full manufacturing account as follows:

Example 6 – Manufacturing account

	£
Opening Stock of Raw Materials	7,000
Purchases of Raw Materials	50,000
Closing Stock of Raw Materials	(10,000)
DIRECT MATERIALS USED	47,000
Direct Labour	97,000
PRIME COST	**144,000**
Manufacturing Overheads	53,000
FACTORY COST	**197,000**
Opening Stock of Work in Progress	8,000
Closing Stock of Work in Progress.	(10,000)
FACTORY COST OF GOODS MANUFACTURED	**195,000**
Opening Stock of Finished Goods	30,000
Closing Stock of Finished Goods	(25,000)
COST OF GOODS SOLD	**200,000**

Activity 6

Reorder the following costs into a manufacturing account format:

	£
Manufacturing Overheads	47,000
Purchases of Raw Materials	60,000
FACTORY COST	**147,000**
Opening Stock of Raw Materials	14,000
Closing Stock of Finished Goods	(70,000)
COST OF GOODS SOLD	**147,000**
PRIME COST	**100,000**
Opening Stock of Work in Progress	42,000
DIRECT MATERIALS USED	64,000
Direct Labour	36,000
Closing Stock of Raw Materials	(10,000)
Closing Stock of Work in Progress.	(32,000)
FACTORY COST OF GOODS MANUFACTURED	**157,000**
Opening Stock of Finished Goods	60,000

4   The materials purchasing cycle in practice

4.1   Introduction

Materials can often form the largest single item of cost for a business so it is essential that the material purchased is the most suitable for the intended purpose.

4.2   Control of purchasing

When goods are purchased they must be ordered, received by the stores department, recorded, issued to the manufacturing department that requires them and eventually paid for. This process needs a great deal of paperwork and strict internal controls.

Internal control consists of full documentation and appropriate authorisation of all transactions, movements of materials and of all requisitions, orders, receipts and payments.

If control is to be maintained over purchasing, it is necessary to ensure that:

- only necessary items are purchased
- orders are placed with the most appropriate supplier after considering price and delivery details
- the goods that are actually received are the goods that were ordered and in the correct quantity
- the price paid for the goods is correct (i.e. what was agreed when the order was placed).

To ensure that all of this takes place requires a reliable system of checking and control.

4.3   Overview of procedures

It is useful to have an overview of the purchasing process.

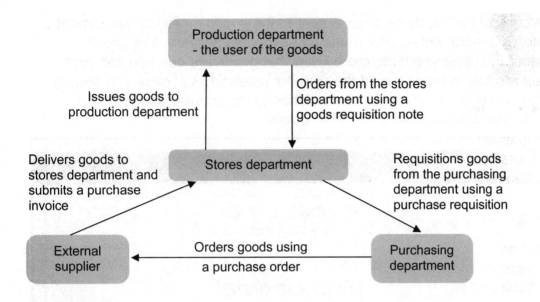

There are many variations of the above system in practice, but it is a fairly typical system and does provide good control over the purchasing and issuing process.

Activity 7 (no feedback)

Your organisation may have a slightly different process to this. See if you can draw a similar diagram illustrating the way your organisation's (or a familiar organisation's) purchasing process works.

4.4 Purchase orders

Purchase orders will be sent to suppliers by the purchasing department. The choice of supplier will depend upon the price, delivery promise, quality of goods and past performance.

The person placing the order must first check that the purchase requisition has been authorised by the appropriate person in the organisation, as a check that the goods are genuinely required by the organisation.

Once the supplier of the goods has been chosen, the purchase price of the goods must be determined. This will either be from the price list of the supplier or from a special quotation of the price by that supplier. The price agreed will be entered on the purchase order together with details of the goods being ordered.

The purchase order must then be authorised by the appropriate person in the organisation before being dispatched to the supplier.

A copy of the purchase order is sent to the goods receiving department or stores department as confirmation of expected delivery. The goods receiving department therefore know that goods are due and can alert appropriate management if they are not received. A copy is also sent to the accounts department to be matched to the supplier's invoice. An example purchase order is shown below.

Example 7

BLACKHILL FILES
742 St Anne's Way, York YO5 4NP
Telephone 01904 27635
Registered in England, No 1457893

PURCHASE ORDER

Printing Unlimited   Order No: 35762
80 New High Street
Exeter   Ref: T. Holmes
EX4 2LP

Date: 22 June 20X4

Please print 25,000 labels at £10.50 from copy supplied per 1,000
Needed by 20 July 20X4
Payment within 30 days of delivery. 2% early settlement discount

Delivery to: As above

4.5   Purchase invoice

The supplier will submit a purchase invoice for goods detailing the amount that we must pay for them and the date that payment is due. The purchase invoice might be included when the goods themselves are delivered, or might be sent after delivery.

The purchase invoice is the primary source of information for recording the quantity and cost of materials purchased.

The person responsible for payment must check that the details of the purchase invoice agree to the purchase order.

This is to ensure that:

- what was ordered was received

- the price charged is that agreed.

Once it is certain that the purchase invoice agrees with the goods that were ordered then the invoice can be authorised for payment.

4.6 Bin cards

The storekeeper must know at any time how much of any item he has in stock. This is done by use of a bin card.

Definition

A **bin card** is a simple record of receipts, issues and balances of stock in hand kept by storekeepers, recorded in quantities of materials stock.

The bin card is a duplication of the quantity information recorded in the stores ledger (see later in this chapter) but storekeepers frequently find that such a ready record is a very useful aid in carrying out their duties.

An example of a bin card for an item of stock is given below.

BIN CARD

Description ....Chipboard......... Location.........Stores......... Code.....D35.....

Maximum 3,000m Minimum....1,000m Reorder level 1,400m Reorder quantity....200m..

	Receipts			Issues		Current stock level	On order		
Date	GRN ref	Quantity	Issue date	Ref	Quantity		Date	Ref	Quantity
30/7/X3	8737	200m				200m	01/8/X3	PO6752	300m
06/7/X3	8748	300m				500m			
			07/8/X9	3771	400m	100m			

The bin card does not have value columns.

4.7 Stores ledger account

As well as the information recorded by the storekeeper on a bin card, the accounts department also keep records for each line of stock, in terms of both quantity and value, and this is known as the stores ledger account.

> ### Q Definition
>
> A stores ledger account records the quantity and value of receipts and issues and the current balance of each item of stock.

The stores ledger account for the item of stock recorded in the bin card earlier in this section is given below:

STORES LEDGER ACCOUNT

Material   Chipboard

Code   D35

Date	Receipts				Issues				Balance		
	GRN Ref	Qty	Price per unit £	Amount £	Issue ref	Qty per unit	Price £	Amount	Qty per unit	Price £	Value £
30/7/X3	8737	200m	2.00	400.00					200	2.00	400.00
06/8/X3	8748	300m	2.00	600.00					500	2.00	1,000.00
07/8/X3					3771	400m	2.00	800.00	100	2.00	200.00

Activity 1

Method	Cost of issue on 19 June	Closing stock at 30 June
FIFO	£2,000	£3,100
LIFO	£2,200	£2,900
AVCO	£2,080	£3,020

Workings

FIFO

- The issue will be made up of all 100 units from June 2, all 200 units from June 3 and 100 of those purchased on June 6 at a price of 1,200/200 = £6 per unit.

- Cost of issue = 400 + 1,000 + 100 × 6 = £2,000

- Total purchases = 400 + 1,000 + 1,200 + 2,500 = £5,100

- Closing stock = 5,100 – 2,000 = £3,100

LIFO

- The issue will be made up of all 200 units from June 6 and all 200 units from June 3.

- Cost of issue = 1,200 + 1,000 = £2,200

- Closing stock = 5,100 – 2,200 = £2,900

AVCO

- Before June 19 we had bought a total of 500 units at a total cost of 400+1,000+1,200 = £2,600

- On average this works out at 2,600/500 = £5.20 per unit

- Thus the cost of the issue will be 400×5.20 = £2,080

- Closing stock = 5,100 – 2,080 = £3,020

Activity 2

Characteristic	FIFO	LIFO	AVCO
• Issues are valued at the most recent purchase cost		☑	
• Stock is valued at the average of the cost of purchases			☑
• Stock is valued at the most recent purchase cost	☑		

Activity 3

	True	False
• FIFO costs issues of stock at the most recent purchase price		☑
• AVCO costs issues of stock at the oldest purchase price		☑
• LIFO costs issues of stock at the oldest purchase price		☑
• FIFO values closing stock at the most recent purchase price	☑	
• LIFO values closing stock at the most recent purchase price		☑
• AVCO values closing stock at the latest purchase price		☑

Activity 4

Element	Total Cost	Unit cost
Materials	£60,000	£4.00
Labour	£75,000	£5.00
Overheads	£60,000	£4.00
Total	£195,000	£13.00

Activity 5

Units	Fixed Costs	Variable Costs	Total Costs	Unit Cost
1,000	£60,000	£2,000	£62,000	£62.00
2,000	£60,000	£4,000	£64,000	£32.00
3,000	£60,000	£6,000	£66,000	£22.00
4,000	£60,000	£8,000	£68,000	£17.00

Activity 6

	£
Opening Stock of Raw Materials	14,000
Purchases of Raw Materials	60,000
Closing Stock of Raw Materials	(10,000)
DIRECT MATERIALS USED	64,000
Direct Labour	36,000
PRIME COST	**100,000**
Manufacturing Overheads	47,000
FACTORY COST	**147,000**
Opening Stock of Work in Progress	42,000
Closing Stock of Work in Progress.	(32,000)
FACTORY COST OF GOODS MANUFACTURED	**157,000**
Opening Stock of Finished Goods	60,000
Closing Stock of Finished Goods	(70,000)
COST OF GOODS SOLD	**147,000**

5 Test your knowledge

Workbook Activity 7

Identify the correct stock valuation method from the characteristic given by putting a tick in the relevant column of the table below.

Characteristic	FIFO	LIFO	AVCO
• Issues are valued at the most recent purchase cost			
• Issues are valued at the oldest purchase cost			
• Issues are valued at the average of the cost of purchases			
• Stock is valued at the most recent purchase cost			
• Stock is valued at the oldest purchase cost			

KAPLAN PUBLISHING

Workbook Activity 8

Adamkus Ltd has the following movements in a certain inventory item into and out of it stores for the month of March:

Date	Receipts		Issues	
	Units	Cost	Units	Cost
March 5	100	£200		
March 12	100	£250		
March 19	200	£600		
March 23			300	
March 27	400	£1,350		

Complete the table below for the issue and closing stock values.

Method	Cost of issue on 23 March	Closing stock at 31 March
FIFO		
LIFO		
AVCO		

Workbook Activity 9

Identify the following statements as either true or false.

Statement	True	False
• FIFO costs issues of stock at the oldest purchase price		
• AVCO values closing stock at the oldest purchase price		
• LIFO costs issues of stock at the oldest purchase price		

Workbook Activity 10

Chiluba Ltd is costing a single product with the following cost details:

Variable Costs per unit

Materials	£10
Labour	£5
Total Fixed Costs	£150,000

Complete the following total cost and unit cost table for a production level of 20,000 units.

Element	Total Cost	Unit cost
Materials	£	£
Labour	£	£
Overheads	£	£
Total	£	£

Workbook Activity 11

Complete the table below showing fixed costs, variable costs, total costs and unit cost at the different levels of production.

Units	Fixed Costs	Variable Costs	Total Costs	Unit Cost
1,000	£200,000	£5,000	£205,000	£205.00
2,000	£	£	£	£
3,000	£	£	£	£
4,000	£	£	£	£

Workbook Activity 12

Reorder the following costs into a manufacturing account format:

	£
FACTORY COST OF GOODS MANUFACTURED	**31,400**
FACTORY COST	**29,400**
PRIME COST	**20,000**
COST OF GOODS SOLD	**29,400**
DIRECT MATERIALS USED	12,800
Manufacturing Overheads	9,400
Purchases of Raw Materials	12,000
Opening Stock of Raw Materials	2,800
Closing Stock of Finished Goods	(14,000)
Opening Stock of Work in Progress	8,400
Direct Labour	7,200
Closing Stock of Raw Materials	(2,000)
Closing Stock of Work in Progress.	(6,400)
Opening Stock of Finished Goods	12,000

Labour costs

4

Introduction

This chapter considers labour costs in more detail.

KNOWLEDGE

Extract income and expenditure details from relevant sources (1.2)

Identify materials, labour and expenses and explain how they are classified and recorded (2.1)

Explain methods for calculating payments for labour (2.7)

SKILLS

Classify, calculate and code cost information for materials, labour and expenses (1.4)

CONTENTS

1 Introduction

1.1 Labour costs

In this unit you need to understand and be able to explain methods of payment for labour to include basic rate (time rate), payment of overtime, payment of bonus and payment by piecework.

You will not be required to have knowledge of specific bonus schemes

1.2 Direct and indirect labour

Just as materials can be classified as direct or indirect so too can labour costs, depending on the job of the employee.

Example

In a manufacturing organisation the factory workers who make the products would be direct labour whereas the factory supervisor would be an example of an indirect labour cost as although he is working in the factory he is not actually making any of the products.

Activity 1

Identify the following statements as true or false by putting a tick in the relevant column of the table below.

Cost	True	False
Direct labour costs can be identified with the goods being made or the service being produced		
Indirect costs vary directly with the level of activity		

1.3 Calculating gross pay

There are two main methods of calculating the gross pay of employees:

- pay employees for the time spent at work (time related pay)
- pay employees for the work actually produced (output related pay).

In addition there may be bonus schemes to be incorporated. These are covered in more detail below.

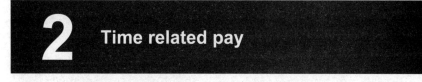

2 Time related pay

2.1 Time related pay

Employees paid under a time related pay method are paid for the hours that they spend at work regardless of the amount of production or output that they achieve in that time. Time related pay employees can be split into two types, **salaried employees** and **hourly rate employees**.

2.2 Salaried employees

🔍 Definition

A **salaried employee** is one whose gross pay is agreed at a fixed amount for a period of time whatever hours that employee works in that period.

This might be expressed as an annual salary such as £18,000 per year or as a weekly rate such as £269.50 per week.

Each organisation will have a set number of hours that are expected to be worked each week, for example a standard working week of 37.5 hours, and salaried employees will be expected to work for at least this number of hours each week.

However if the salaried employee works for more than the standard number of hours for the week then the employment agreement may specify that overtime payments are to be made for the additional hours.

2.3 Hourly rate employees

🔍 Definition

An **hourly rate employee** is one who is paid a set hourly rate for each hour that he works.

These employees are paid for the actual number of hours of attendance in a period, usually a week. A rate of pay will be set for each hour of attendance.

2.4 Overtime

🔍 Definition

Overtime is the number of hours worked by an employee which is greater than the number of hours set by the organisation as the working week.

It is common that employees that work overtime are paid an additional amount per hour for those extra hours.

2.5 Overtime premium

🔍 Definition

Overtime premium is the amount over and above the normal hourly rate that employees are paid for overtime hours.

💡 Example

An employee's basic week is 40 hours at a rate of pay of £8 per hour. Overtime is paid at 'time and a half'. The employee works a 45-hour week. What is the total gross pay for this employee for the week?

	£
Basic hours 40 × £8	320.00
Overtime 5 × £12	60.00
	———
	380.00
	———

The overtime payment can be split between the basic rate element and the overtime premium:

	£
Basic pay 5 × £8	40.00
Overtime premium 5 × £4	20.00
	———
	60.00
	———

Activity 2

Singh Ltd pays a time-rate of £12 per hour to its direct labour for a standard 35 hour week. Any of the labour force working in excess of 35 hours is paid an overtime rate of £15 per hour.

Calculate the gross wage for the week for the workers in the table below.

Worker	Hours worked	Basic wage £	Overtime £	Gross wage £
J. Patel	35			
D. Smith	38			
S. O'Leary	42			

3   Output related pay

Output related pay is also known as payment by results or piecework. This is a direct alternative to time related pay.

Definition

Payment by results or piecework is where a fixed amount is paid per unit of output achieved irrespective of the time spent.

3.1   Advantages of payment by results

As far as an employee is concerned, payment by results means that they can earn whatever they wish within certain parameters. The harder they work and the more units they produce the higher the wage they will earn.

From the employer's point of view higher production or output can also be encouraged with a system of differential piecework (see later in chapter).

3.2 Problems with payment by results

There are two main problems associated with payment by results. One is the problem of accurate recording of the actual output produced. The amount claimed to be produced determines the amount of pay and, therefore, is potentially open to abuse unless it can be adequately supervised. A system of job sheets and checking of job sheets needs to be in place.

The second problem is that of the maintenance of the quality of the work. If the employee is paid by the amount that is produced then the temptation might be to produce more units but of a lower quality.

For these reasons basic piecework systems are rare in practice – variations of these systems are used instead.

Activity 3

Stizgt Ltd uses a piecework method to pay labour in one of its factories. The rate used is 90p per unit produced.

Calculate the gross wage for the week for the workers in the table below.

Worker	Units produced in week	Gross wage £
S. McHenry	200 units	
D. Weaver	320 units	
S. Hasina	250 units	

3.3 Piece rate with guarantee

A **piece rate with guarantee** gives the employee some security if the employer does not provide enough work in a particular period. The way that the system works is that if an employee's earnings for the amount of units produced in the period are lower than the guaranteed amount then the guaranteed amount is paid instead.

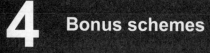

Activity 4

Fernando is paid £3.00 for every unit that he produces but he has a guaranteed wage of £28.00 per eight hour day. In a particular week he produces the following number of units:

Monday   12 units

Tuesday   14 units

Wednesday   9 units

Thursday   14 units

Friday   8 units

Calculate Fernando's wage for this week.

4   Bonus schemes

Bonuses may be paid to employees for a variety of reasons. An individual employee, a department, a division or the entire organisation may have performed particularly well and it is felt by the management that a bonus is due to some or all of the employees.

4.1   Basic principle of bonuses

The basic principle of a bonus payment is that the employee is rewarded for any additional income or savings in cost to the organisation. This may be, for example, because the employee has managed to save a certain amount of time on the production of a product or a number of products. This time saving will save the organisation money and the amount saved will tend to be split between the organisation and the employee on some agreed basis. The amount paid to the employee/employees is known as the bonus.

4.2   Method of payment

The typical bonus payable will often depend on the method of payment of the employee. The calculation and payment of bonuses will differ for salaried employees, employees paid by results and employees paid on a time rate basis.

Activity 5

Meidani Ltd uses a time-rate method with bonus to pay its direct labour in one of its factories. The time-rate used is £10 per hour and a worker is expected to produce 6 units an hour, anything over this and the worker is paid a bonus of £2 per unit.

Calculate the gross wage for the week for the workers in the table below.

Worker	Hours worked	Units produced	Basic wage £	Bonus £	Gross wage £
J. Klestil	35	220			
C. Zemin	35	205			
J. Chirac	40	240			

Activity 6

Identify the labour payment method by putting a tick in the relevant column of the table below.

Payment method	Time-rate	Piece-rate	Time-rate plus bonus
Labour is paid based on the production achieved			
Labour is paid extra if an agreed level of output is exceeded			
Labour is paid according to hours worked			

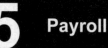 **Activity 7**

Identify one **advantage** for each labour payment method by putting a tick in the relevant column of the table below.

Payment method	Time-rate	Piece-rate	Time-rate plus bonus
Assured level of remuneration for employee			
Employee earns more if they work more efficiently than expected			
Assured level of remuneration and reward for working efficiently			

5 Payroll

5.1 Initial recording of gross pay

The initial calculation and recording of gross pay for employees will be done in the payroll department. This department will then also calculate any PAYE and NIC and any further deductions in order to determine the net pay for each employee for the period.

5.2 Coding of labour costs

Payroll calculations are necessary in order to pay employees the correct amounts and to record the correct gross pay figure for financial accounting purposes.

However for cost accounting purposes more detail is needed. It is important that the gross pay of each employee is coded so that it is recognised by the correct production or service cost centre.

In some instances an employee's clock card or time sheet might show that he worked for different cost centres during the period and therefore the gross pay must be broken down into the amount to be recognised by each cost centre and correctly coded as such.

5.3 Service cost centre employees

The employees of a manufacturing organisation do not all work for cost centres that actually produce the products. Many employees will work in service cost centres such as stores, the canteen, the accounts department and the sales division.

Costs need to be recognised by each of these service cost centres and therefore the gross pay of these employees must also be coded to show which cost centre they have worked for in the period.

5.4 Employers' National Insurance Contributions

When an employer pays the wages or salaries of an employee it must also pay a proportion of that amount to the Inland Revenue in the form of the Employer's National Insurance Contribution (NIC). This is a necessary cost of employing workers and is therefore part of the cost of labour for an employer.

5.5 Coding labour costs

The labour costs of the employees of an organisation will need to be coded to the appropriate cost centre but also coded according to the correct classification. The total labour cost of an employee can be made up of the following:

- Basic pay
- Overtime premium
- Bonus
- Employers' NIC.

In many organisations only the basic pay for all hours worked in the period and the employers' NIC are treated as a labour cost. In contrast the overtime premium and any bonus payments are treated as expenses rather than labour costs. It is important to ensure that the person coding the labour costs has fully understood the organisation's policies on these matters.

6 Sources of information

6.1 Documentation and procedures to record labour costs

When an employee joins an organisation it must record details of the employee, their job and pay. This is done by the personnel department in the individual employee's personnel record.

Details that might be kept about an employee are as follows:

- full name, address and date of birth

- personal details such as marital status and emergency contact name and address

- National Insurance number

- previous employment history

- educational details

- professional qualifications

- date of joining organisation

- employee number or code

- clock number issued

- job title and department

- rate of pay agreed

- holiday details agreed

- bank details if salary is to be paid directly into bank account

- amendments to any of the details above (such as increases in agreed rates of pay)

- date of termination of employment (when this takes place) and reasons for leaving.

6.2 Employee record of attendance

On any particular day an employee may be at work, on holiday, absent due to sickness or absent for some other reason. A record must be kept of these details for each day.

This information about an employee's attendance will come from various sources such as clock cards, time sheets, job sheets, and job cards.

7 Summary

In this chapter we looked at different ways of calculating a labour cost. Make sure you can distinguish between time-rate, piece-rate and bonus schemes.

Answers to chapter activities

Activity 1

Cost	True	False
Direct labour costs can be identified with the goods being made or the service being produced	☑	
Indirect costs vary directly with the level of activity		☑

Activity 2

Worker	Hours worked	Basic wage £	Overtime £	Gross wage £
J. Patel	35	420	0	420
D. Smith	38	420	45	465
S. O'Leary	42	420	105	525

Activity 3

Worker	Units produced in week	Gross wage £
S. McHenry	200 units	180.00
D. Weaver	320 units	288.00
S. Hasina	250 units	225.00

Activity 4

Fernando would be paid £176.

Working:

Total weekly wage

	£
Monday (12 × 3)	36
Tuesday (14 × 3)	42
Wednesday (guarantee)	28
Thursday (14 × 3)	42
Friday (guarantee)	28
	176

The payment of a guaranteed amount is not a bonus for good work but simply an additional payment required if the amount of production is below a certain level.

Activity 5

Worker	Hours worked	Units produced	Basic wage £	Bonus £	Gross wage £
J. Klestil	35	220	350	20	370
C. Zemin	35	205	350	0	350
J. Chirac	40	240	400	0	400

Working:

- Basic wage = £10 × hours worked

- In 35 hours we would expect 35 × 6 = 210 units.
  J Klestil exceeded this by 10 units, giving a bonus of 10 × 2 = £20
  C. Zemin did not, so received no bonus.

- In 40 hours we would expect 40 × 6 = 240 units.
  J. Chirac did not exceed this, so received no bonus.

Activity 6

Payment method	Time-rate	Piece-rate	Time-rate plus bonus
Labour is paid based on the production achieved		☑	
Labour is paid extra if an agreed level of output is exceeded			☑
Labour is paid according to hours worked	☑		

Activity 7

Payment method	Time-rate	Piece-rate	Time-rate plus bonus
Assured level of remuneration for employee	☑		
Employee earns more if they work more efficiently than expected		☑	
Assured level of remuneration and reward for working efficiently			☑

8 Test your knowledge

Workbook Activity 8

Karimov Ltd pays a time-rate of £10 per hour to its direct labour for a standard 37 hour week. Any of the labour force working in excess of 37 hours is paid "time and a half".

Calculate the gross wage for the week for the workers in the table below.

Worker	Hours worked	Basic wage £	Overtime £	Gross wage £
M. Khan	42			
D. Murphy	37			
K. Ng	40			

Workbook Activity 9

Gibson plc uses a piecework method to pay labour to make clothing in one of its factories. The rate used is £2.50 per garment completed.

Calculate the gross wage for the week for the workers in the table below.

Worker	Units produced in week	Gross wage £
H. Potter	100 units	
T. Riddle	130 units	
S. Snape	175 units	

Workbook Activity 10

Leonid is paid £5.00 for every unit that he produces but he has a guaranteed minimum wage of £25.00 per day.

Calculate Leonid's wage for this week by filling in the following table:

Day	Units produced	Gross wage £
Monday	4 units	
Tuesday	6 units	
Wednesday	9 units	
Thursday	3 units	
Friday	8 units	
Total	30 units	

Workbook Activity 11

Legolas Ltd uses a time-rate method with bonus to pay its direct labour in one of its factories. The time-rate used is £12 per hour and a worker is expected to produce 10 units an hour, anything over this and the worker is paid a bonus of £1 per unit.

Calculate the gross wage for the week for the workers in the table below.

Worker	Hours worked	Units produced	Basic wage £	Bonus £	Gross wage £
L. Aragon	37	375			
T. Ent	35	360			
K. Theodin	42	410			

Budgeting

Introduction

This chapter looks briefly at budgeting before focussing on variances and how they can be used to help control an organisation.

KNOWLEDGE
Identify sources of income and expenditure information for historic, current and forecast periods (1.4)

SKILLS
Compare actual and expected costs (2.1)
Identify any discrepancies and refer or report to an appropriate person (2.2)

CONTENTS
1 Budgeting
2 Identifying budgeted costs
3 Variances

1 Budgeting

1.1 Introduction

In this unit you need to have a brief knowledge of budgeting as an aid to planning and control but this need only be at a basic level.

You will not be required to explain the nature of budgeted costs in any great detail, but will be required to identify budgeted costs and to compare with actual costs by using variances.

1.2 What is budgeting?

Budgets set out the costs and revenues that are expected to be incurred or earned in future periods.

For example, if you are planning to take a holiday, you will probably have a budgeted amount that you can spend. This budget will determine where you go and for how long.

Most organisations prepare budgets for the business as a whole. The following budgets may also be prepared by organisations:

- Departmental budgets
- Functional budgets (for sales, production, expenditure and so on).
- Income statements (in order to determine the expected future profits).
- Cash budgets (in order to determine future cash flows).

1.3 Budgetary control

As stated in chapter 1, the main reason for budgeting is to help managers control the business.

The budget contains a mixture of what you think will happen and what you intend to make happen.

For example, suppose we think we will be able to sell 100 units in June (a sales forecast) and therefore plan to make 100 units in May (a production budget). This means we need to buy 200kg of material X at an expected cost of £5 per kg (a materials purchases budget)

This then gives a benchmark against which we can evaluate actual performance.

For example, what if we only sold 90 units, or used 210kg of material or it cost £5.50/kg not £5.

Any difference or variance can then be investigated to identify the cause. Once we know this we can take appropriate action.

For example, if the price of materials was higher because our normal supplier put their prices up, then we could consider trying to find another supplier.

1.4 Other reasons for budgeting

Other reasons for budgeting include the following:

- **Authorisation**

  A budget may act as a formal authorisation to a manager to spend a given amount on specified activities.

- **Forecasting**

  Forecasting refers to the prediction of events over which little or no control is exercised. Some parts of all budgets are, therefore, based on forecasts.

- **Planning**

  Planning is an attempt to shape the future by a conscious effort to influence those factors which are open to control.

- **Communication and co-ordination**

  Budgets communicate plans to managers responsible for carrying them out. They also ensure co-ordination between managers of sub-units so that each is aware of the others' requirements.

- **Motivation**

  Budgets are often intended to motivate managers to perform in line with organisational plans and objectives.

- **Evaluation**

  The performance of managers and organisational units is often evaluated by reference to budgetary targets.

2 Identifying budgeted costs

2.1 Introduction

Within the basic costing unit you will need to be able to calculate total and unit costs at different activity levels.

2.2 Cost behaviour

When calculating budgeted costs remember to distinguish between variable costs and fixed costs

- Fixed costs will remain constant for each activity level
- Variable costs will increase in line with activity levels

Example 1

Complete the table below showing budgeted fixed costs, variable costs, total costs and unit cost at the different possible budgeted levels of production

Units	Fixed costs	Variable costs	Total costs	Unit cost
100	400	200	600	6.00
200				
300				

Solution

Units	Fixed costs	Variable costs	Total costs	Unit cost
100	400	200	600	6.00
200	400	400	800	4.00
300	400	600	1,000	3.33

Notes: You may recall doing similar calculations in chapter 1

- Fixed costs do not change

- To get variable costs either

  (a) Simply prorate – e.g. to go from 100 to 300 units the volume has trebled , so treble the cost: 3 × 200 = £600, or

  (b) First calculate the variable cost per unit = 200/100 = £2 per unit. This can be used to work out other variable costs, so for 300 units the variable cost will be 300 × 2 = £600

- Total costs are simply the sum of fixed and variable

- To get the unit cost, divide the total cost by the number of units. So for 200 units the unit cost = £800/200 = £4 per unit.

Activity 1

Complete the table below showing budgeted fixed costs, variable costs, total costs and unit cost at the different budgeted levels of production

Units	Fixed costs	Variable costs	Total costs	Expected Unit cost
1,000	£2,400	£600	£3,000	£3.00
2,000				
3,000				
4,000				

Activity 2

Moussa Ltd is budgeting for the costs of a single product which has the following cost details:

Variable costs per unit

- Materials   £5 per unit
- Labour   £8 per unit

Total fixed costs   £60,000

Complete the following budgeted total cost and unit cost table for a production level of 30,000 units

Element	Total cost £	Unit cost £
Materials		
Labour		
Overheads		
Total		

Activity 3

Barak Ltd makes a single product and has estimated the following expected costs for a budgeted production level of 12,000 units:

- Materials   3,600kg at £5 per kg
- Labour   600 hours at £12 per hour
- Overheads   £60,000

Complete the table below to show the expected unit cost at the production level of 12,000 units

Element	Unit cost £
Materials	
Labour	
Overheads	
Total	

3 Variances

3.1   What is a variance?

The difference between actual and expected (or budgeted) cost is known as a variance.

- A **favourable** variance ("Fav") is when the actual cost is lower than expected and
- An **adverse** variance ("Adv") is when actual cost is higher than expected.

3.2   How to calculate a variance

For Basic Costing the only calculation required will be a comparison of actual to expected cost.

Example 2

Fujimori Ltd has produced a performance report detailing budgeted and actual material cost for last month.

Calculate the amount of the variance and then determine whether it is adverse or favourable by putting a tick in the relevant column of the table below.

Cost type	Budget £	Actual £	Variance £	Adv.	Fav.
Materials	24,500	26,200			

Solution

Cost type	Budget £	Actual £	Variance £	Adv.	Fav.
Materials	24,500	26,200	1,700	☑	

Notes:

- Variance = 26,200 – 24,500 = £1,700
- The variance is adverse as the actual cost is higher than budgeted

Activity 4

Kagame Ltd has produced a performance report detailing budgeted and actual cost for last month.

Calculate the amount of the variance for each cost type and then determine whether it is adverse or favourable by putting a tick in the relevant column of the table below.

Cost type	Budget £	Actual £	Variance £	Adv.	Fav.
Materials	56,000	49,500			
Labour	64,000	65,200			
Overheads	150,000	148,500			

Activity 5

Identify the following statements as being true or false by putting a tick in the relevant column of the table below.

Statement	True	False
A variance is the difference between budgeted and actual cost		
A favourable variance means budgeted costs are greater than actual costs		
An adverse variance means you have made a saving compared to budgeted costs		

3.3 Evaluating the significance of a variance

Management do not want to waste time investigating small variances, so will set criteria for deciding what makes a variance large enough to report and investigate.

For example,

- "Only investigate variances bigger than £500"

- "Only investigate variances bigger that 5% of budget"

If using a percentage measure then the amount of the variance that exceeds the cut-off percentage is known as the "discrepancy".

Example 3

Antrobus Ltd has produced a performance report detailing budgeted and actual material cost for last month. Any variance in excess of 10% of budget is deemed to be significant and should be reviewed.

Calculate the amount of the variance and then determine whether it is significant by putting a tick in the relevant column of the table below.

Cost type	Budget £	Actual £	Variance £	Significant	Not significant
Labour	5,600	5,200			

Solution

Cost type	Budget £	Actual £	Variance £	Significant	Not significant
Labour	5,600	5,200	400		☑

Notes:

- Variance = 5,200 – 5,600 = £400

- As a % of budget this gives (400/5,600) × 100% = 7.1%, which is less than 10%, so the variance is deemed not significant.

Activity 6

Guterres Ltd has produced a performance report detailing budgeted and actual cost for this month. Any variance in excess of 5% of budget is deemed to be significant and should be reported to the relevant manager.

Examine the variances in the table below and indicate whether they are significant or not by putting a tick in the relevant column.

Cost type	Budget £	Variance £	Significant	Not significant
Direct materials	26,000	1,200		
Direct Labour	35,000	2,000		
Production overheads	15,000	1,100		
Selling costs	2,000	90		

3.4 Assigning responsibility for variances

Once variances have been identified, we need to consider who would be most interested in it. This usually means the manager who could be held **responsible** for the variance or who could have caused it.

For example,

- material variances might want to be seen by the production manager and purchasing manager,

- labour variances might want to be seen by the production manager and HR manager, and

- expense variances might want to be seen by the administration manager.

Note: The reasons why these managers would want to see these variances and the causes of any variances are not examined.

 **Activity 7**

The performance report for Kofi plc shows that the following cost variances were significant

- Direct Labour Cost

- Selling and distribution costs

These variances needed to be reported to the relevant managers for review and appropriate action if required.

Identify from the table below a relevant manager for each significant variance to whom the performance report should be sent.

Variance	Manager
Direct labour cost	
Selling and distribution costs	

Note: You may select from the following managers:

- Production manager
- Purchasing manager
- Marketing manager
- IT manager

4 Summary

In this chapter we looked briefly at budgeting, how to calculate budget costs and the basics of variance analysis.

Answers to chapter activities

Activity 1

Units	Fixed costs	Variable costs	Total costs	Unit cost
1,000	£2,400	£600	£3,000	£3.00
2,000	£2,400	£1,200	£3,600	£1.80
3,000	£2,400	£1,800	£4,200	£1.40
4,000	£2,400	£2,400	£4,800	£1.20

Activity 2

Element	Total cost £	Unit cost £
Materials	150,000	5
Labour	240,000	8
Overheads	60,000	2
Total	450,000	15

Activity 3

Element	Unit cost £
Materials	1.50
Labour	0.60
Overheads	5.00
Total	7.10

Notes:

- To get material costs per unit, either

    (a) Calculate the total material cost (3,600 × 5 = 18,000) and divide this by the number of units: 18,000 ÷ 12,000 = £1.50 per unit, or

    (b) First calculate the usage per unit = 3,600/12,000 = 0.3kg per unit. The cost per unit is then 0.3kg at £5 per kg = £1.50

- To get labour costs per unit, either

    (a) Calculate the total labour cost (600 × 12=7,200) and divide this by the number of units: 7,200 ÷ 12,000 = £0.60 per unit, or

    (b) First calculate the time per unit = 600/12,000 = 0.05 hours per unit. The cost per unit is then 0.05 hours at £12 per hour = £0.60

- To get the overhead unit cost, divide the total cost by the number of units = 60,000/12,000 = £5 per unit

Activity 4

Cost type	Budget £	Actual £	Variance £	Adv.	Fav.
Materials	56,000	49,500	6,500		☑
Labour	64,000	65,200	1,200	☑	
Overheads	150,000	148,500	1,500		☑

Activity 5

Statement	True	False
A variance is the difference between budgeted and actual cost	☑	
A favourable variance means budgeted costs are greater than actual costs	☑	
An adverse variance means you have made a saving compared to budgeted costs		☑

Activity 6

Cost type	Budget £	Variance £	Significant	Not significant
Direct materials	26,000	1,200		☑
Direct Labour	35,000	2,000	☑	
Production overheads	15,000	1,100	☑	
Selling costs	2,000	90		☑

Workings

- Materials   (1,200/26,000) × 100   = 4.6%
- Labour   (2,000/35,000) × 100   = 5.7%
- Overheads   (1,100/15,000) × 100   = 7.3%
- Selling costs (90/2,000) × 100   = 4.5%

Activity 7

Variance	Manager
Direct labour cost	Production manager
Selling and distribution costs	Marketing manager

5 Test your knowledge

Workbook Activity 8

Ben Ali Ltd has produced a performance report detailing budgeted and actual cost for last month.

Calculate the amount of the variance for each cost type and then determine whether it is adverse or favourable by putting a tick in the relevant column of the table below.

Cost type	Budget £	Actual £	Variance £	Adv.	Fav.
Materials	24,500	25,000			
Labour	15,000	14,950			
Overheads	120,600	120,000			

Workbook Activity 9

Identify the following statements as being true or false by putting a tick in the relevant column of the table below.

Statement	True	False
A variance is the difference between actual and budgeted cost		
A variance is the average of actual and budgeted cost		
A favourable variance means this cost element would reduce profit compared to budget		
An adverse variance means you have made a saving compared to budgeted costs		

Workbook Activity 10

Ionatana Ltd has produced a performance report detailing budgeted and actual material cost for last month. Any variance in excess of 6% of budget is deemed to be significant and should be reviewed.

Calculate the amount of the variance and then determine whether it is significant by putting a tick in the relevant column of the table below.

Cost type	Budget	Actual	Variance	Significant?	
	£	£	£	Yes	No
Direct Labour	10,000	9,500			
Direct Materials	13,000	15,200			
Production overheads	24,000	25,120			
Administration costs	35,000	32,400			
Selling and distribution costs	45,000	49,260			

Workbook Activity 11

Identify from the options below a relevant manager for each significant variance to whom the performance report should be sent.

Variance	Manager
Direct labour cost	
Selling and distribution costs	
Cost of materials used	
Cost of materials purchased	

Note: You may select from the following managers:

- Production manager
- Purchasing manager
- Marketing manager
- IT manager

WORKBOOK ACTIVITIES
ANSWERS

Workbook Activities Answers

1   Cost Classification

Workbook Activity 11

Characteristic	Financial Accounting	Management Accounting
Content can include forecasts		☑
Looks mainly at historical information	☑	
Format must conform to statute and accounting standards	☑	
Any format that seems useful can be used		☑
Mainly produced to help managers run and control the business		☑
Would be used by potential investors thinking of buying shares	☑	
Produced for shareholders	☑	

Workbook Activity 12

Cost	Production	Admin.	Distribution
Purchases of wood to make chairs	☑		
Depreciation of delivery vans			☑
HR director's bonus		☑	
Salaries of production workers	☑		
Electricity bill for workshop	☑		
Insurance of sales team laptops			☑

Workbook Activity 13

Cost	Direct	Indirect
Travelling costs for when staff visit clients	☑	
Rechargeable accountants' time	☑	
Office heating costs		☑
Recruitment costs		☑
Accountants' time recorded as "general admin." on time sheets		☑

Workbook Activity 14

Cost	Fixed	Variable	Semi-variable
Sales staff pay			☑
Motor oil used in servicing		☑	
Depreciation of premises	☑		
Mechanics' pay (salaried)	☑		
Electricity			☑

2 Coding of costs and income

Workbook Activity 3

Product	Code
Boys shoes, brown leather uppers, rubber soles, size 4	3314240
Ladies slippers, green suede uppers, rubber soles, size 4½	2653245
Girls shoes, burgundy leather uppers, leather soles, size 3½.	4364135

(i)   Boys shoes, brown leather uppers, rubber soles, size 4.

Code: 3   ③   ①   ④   ②   4   ⓪

| These are given in the question | Derived from first code illustrated in question | As a half-size is shown in codes 1 and 2 in question 5, it is assumed 0 can represent whole sized |

(ii) Ladies slippers, green felt uppers, rubber soles, size 4½.

Code   2   (6)   5   (3)   (2)   (4)   (5)

Derived from first code illustrated in question

This was given in the question

As shown in code 1 and 2 in the question

(iii) Girls shoes, burgundy leather uppers, leather soles, size 3½.

Code   4   (3)   6   (4)   (1)   3   5

Derived from second code in question

Workbook Activity 4

Transaction	Code
Factory rent in the Dublin factory.	1120201
Administration telephone costs incurred in Lagos.	1224203
Salesman in Hong Kong entertaining an overseas visitor	1821205
Marketing brochures ordered in London	1021202

3 Materials and stock

Workbook Activity 7

Identify the correct stock valuation method from the characteristic given by putting a tick in the relevant column of the table below.

Characteristic	FIFO	LIFO	AVCO
• Issues are valued at the most recent purchase cost		☑	
• Issues are valued at the oldest purchase cost	☑		
• Issues are valued at the average of the cost of purchases			☑
• Stock is valued at the most recent purchase cost	☑		
• Stock is valued at the oldest purchase cost		☑	

Workbook Activity 8

Method	Cost of issue on 23 March	Closing stock at 31 March
FIFO	750	1,650
LIFO	850	1,550
AVCO	787.50	1,612.50

Workings

FIFO

- The issue will be made up of all 100 units from March 5, all 100 units from March 12 and 100 of those purchased on March 19 at a price of 600/200 = £3 per unit.
- Cost of issue = 200 + 250 + 100 × 3 = £750
- Total purchases = 200 + 250 + 600 + 1,350 = £2,400
- Closing stock = 2,400 – 750 = £1,650

LIFO

- The issue will be made up of all 200 units from March 19 and 100 units from March 12 at a price of 250/100 = £2.50 per unit.
- Cost of issue = 600 + 100 × 2.50 = £850
- Closing stock = 2,400 – 850 = £1,550

AVCO

- Before March 23 we had bought a total of 400 units at a total cost of 200 + 250 + 600 = £1,050
- On average this works out at 1,050/400 = £2.625 per unit
- Thus the cost of the issue will be 300 × 2.625 = £787.50
- Closing stock = 2,400 – 787.5 = £1,612.50

Workbook Activity 9

Identify the following statements as either true or false.

Statement	True	False
• FIFO costs issues of stock at the oldest purchase price	☑	
• AVCO values closing stock at the oldest purchase price		☑
• LIFO costs issues of stock at the oldest purchase price		☑

Workbook Activity 10

Element	Total Cost	Unit cost
Materials	£200,000	£10.00
Labour	£100,000	£5.00
Overheads	£150,000	£7.50
Total	£450,000	£22.50

Workbook Activity 11

Units	Fixed Costs	Variable Costs	Total Costs	Unit Cost
1,000	£200,000	£5,000	£205,000	£205.00
2,000	£200,000	£10,000	£210,000	£105.00
3,000	£200,000	£15,000	£215,000	£71.67
4,000	£200,000	£20,000	£220,000	£55.00

Workbook Activity 12

	£
Opening Stock of Raw Materials	2,800
Purchases of Raw Materials	12,000
Closing Stock of Raw Materials	(2,000)
DIRECT MATERIALS USED	12,800
Direct Labour	7,200
PRIME COST	**20,000**
Manufacturing Overheads	9,400
FACTORY COST	**29,400**
Opening Stock of Work in Progress	8,400
Closing Stock of Work in Progress.	(6,400)
FACTORY COST OF GOODS MANUFACTURED	**31,400**
Opening Stock of Finished Goods	12,000
Closing Stock of Finished Goods	(14,000)
COST OF GOODS SOLD	**29,400**

4 Labour costs

 **Workbook Activity 8**

Worker	Hours worked	Basic wage £	Overtime £	Gross wage £
M. Khan	42	370	75	445
D. Murphy	37	370	0	370
K. Ng	40	370	45	415

Workbook Activity 9

Worker	Units produced in week	Gross wage £
H. Potter	100 units	250.00
T. Riddle	130 units	325.00
S. Snape	175 units	437.50

Workbook Activity 10

Day	Units produced	Gross wage £
Monday	4 units	25
Tuesday	6 units	30
Wednesday	9 units	45
Thursday	3 units	25
Friday	8 units	40
Total	30 units	165

Workbook Activity 11

Worker	Hours worked	Units produced	Basic wage £	Bonus £	Gross wage £
L. Aragon	37	375	444	5	449
T. Ent	35	360	420	10	430
K. Theodin	42	410	504	0	504

5 Budgeting

Workbook Activity 8

Cost type	Budget £	Actual £	Variance £	Adv.	Fav.
Materials	24,500	25,000	500	☑	
Labour	15,000	14,950	50		☑
Overheads	120,600	120,000	600		☑

Workbook Activity 9

Statement	True	False
A variance is the difference between actual and budgeted cost	☑	
A variance is the average of actual and budgeted cost		☑
A favourable variance means this cost element would reduce profit compared to budget		☑
An adverse variance means you have made a saving compared to budgeted costs		☑

Workbook Activity 10

Cost type	Budget £	Actual £	Variance £	Significant? Yes	No
Direct Labour	10,000	9,500	500		☑
Direct Materials	13,000	15,200	2,200	☑	
Production overheads	24,000	25,120	1,120		☑
Administration costs	35,000	32,400	2,600	☑	
Selling and distribution costs	45,000	49,260	4,260	☑	

Workbook Activity 11

Variance	Manager
Direct labour cost	Production manager
Selling and distribution costs	Marketing manager
Cost of materials used	Production manager*
Cost of materials purchased	Purchasing manager

* You could argue that purchasing manager is also a valid answer here

KAPLAN PUBLISHING

MOCK ASSESSMENT

1 Mock Assessment Questions

SECTION 1

Task 1.1

The table below lists costs which have been grouped by different businesses. Classify each grouping by putting a tick in the relevant column of the table below.

Groups of costs	Cost unit	Cost centre
• The catering order for one client in a catering company		
• The parts department of a car dealership		
• A particular beauty treatment in a beauty salon		
• The legal department of a newspaper group		

Task 1.2

Ruggles is a fabric manufacturer.

Classify the following costs by element (materials, labour or overheads) by putting a tick in the relevant column of the table below.

Cost	Materials	Labour	Overheads
• Yarn used in weaving fabrics			
• Rent of weaving looms			
• Salary of the weaving supervisor			
• Wages of machinists in the hand finishing department			

Task 1.3

Pet Care Lid is a veterinary practice.

Classify the following costs by nature (direct or indirect) by putting a tick in the relevant column of the table below.

Cost	Direct	Indirect
• Antiseptic lotion used on injuries		
• Wages of receptionist		
• Wages of veterinary nurse		
• Insurance of premises		

Task 1.4

Identify the following statements as either true or false by putting a tick in the relevant column of the table below.

	True	False
• Cost codes simplify comparison of individual items of expense		
• Cost codes increase the variations in classification		
• Cost codes often incorporate check codes within the main code to check the accuracy of the postings.		

KAPLAN PUBLISHING

Task 1.5

Pet Care Ltd operates a veterinary practice and uses a coding system for its elements of cost (materials, labour or overheads) and then further classifies each element by nature (direct or indirect cost) as below. So, for example, the code for direct materials is A100.

Element of Cost	Code	Nature of Cost	Code
Materials	A	Direct	100
		Indirect	200
Labour	B	Direct	100
		Indirect	200
Overheads	C	Direct	100
		Indirect	200

Code the following costs, extracted from invoices and payroll, using the table below.

Cost	Code
• Stationary materials used by receptionist	
• Medicines prescribed to pets	
• Salary of veterinary nurse	
• Legal costs to negotiate lease of new premises	
• Wages of receptionist	

Task 1.6

Boardwise Ltd produces handmade skateboards and snowboards.

Classify the following costs by function (production, administration, or selling and distribution) by putting a tick in the relevant column of the table below.

Cost	Production	Administration	Selling and Distribution
• Purchases of board wheels			
• Depreciation of packing department machinery			
• Salaries of carpenters in the workshop			
• Insurance of accounting department computer network			

Task 1.7

Canvas Ltd manufactures and sells tents.

Classify the following costs as either fixed or variable by putting a tick in the relevant column of the table below.

Costs	Fixed	Variable
• Tent pegs		
• Salaries of production supervisors		
• Wages of production workers paid by a piece rate method		
• Lease of a machine used in production		

Task 1.8

Redbook Ltd is a printing company.

Classify the following costs by their behaviour (fixed, variable, or semi-variable) by putting a tick in the relevant column of the table below.

Cost	Fixed	Variable	Semi-variable
• Labour costs paid on a piecework basis			
• Ink used in the printing process			
• Finance officer's salary for the year			
• Machine lease costs which includes an element based on usage			

Task 1.9

Identify the following statements as either true or false by putting a tick in the relevant column of the table below.

Statement	True	False
• The prime cost of a unit includes material, labour and allocated overhead per unit		
• Selling and distribution costs are not included in total production overhead		
• Cost of sales will include the cost of sales staff salaries		
• Depreciation of a delivery van would be included in distribution costs		

Task 1.10

Holland Ltd is costing a single product which has the following cost details

Variable Costs per unit

Materials	£4
Labour	£6
Total Fixed Costs	£63,300

Complete the following total cost and unit cost table for a production level of 15,000 units.

Element	Total Cost	Unit Cost
Materials	£	£
Labour	£	£
Overheads	£	£
Total	£	£

Task 1.11

Mombok Ltd, a computer manufacturer, uses a numerical coding structure based on one profit centre and three cost centres as outlined below. Each code has a sub-code so each transaction will be coded as ***/***

Profit/Cost Centre	Code	Sub-classification	Sub-code
Sales	100	European Sales	100
		US Sales	200
Production	200	Direct Cost	100
		Indirect Cost	200
Administration	300	Direct Cost	100
		Indirect Cost	200
Selling and Distribution	400	Direct Cost	100
		Indirect Cost	200

Code the following revenue and expense transactions, which have been extracted from purchase invoices, sales invoices and payroll, using the table below.

Transaction	Code
• Accounts department salaries	
• Packing boxes for computers	
• Sales to France, Europe	
• Package and posting costs to individual customers	
• Graphics cards for computers	
• Factory canteen wages	

Task 1.12

Mohito Ltd makes a single product and for a production level of 25,000 units has the following cost details:

Materials 4000 litres at £15 per litre

Labour 6000 hours at £12.50 an hour

Overheads   £55,000

Complete the table below to show the unit cost at the production level of 25,000 units.

Element	Unit Cost
Materials	£
Labour	£
Overheads	£
Total	£

SECTION 2

Task 2.1

Identify the following statements about employee payment methods as either true or false by putting a tick in the relevant column of the table below.

	True	False
• Employees paid under a time related pay method are paid a fixed amount per unit of output achieved irrespective of the time spent		
• A problem with the piece rate payment method can be maintenance of the quality of the work.		
• An advantage of the piece rate payment method is that the employee earns more if they work more efficiently than expected		
• A salaried employee is one who is paid a set hourly rate for each hour that they work.		

Task 2.2

Identify the correct stock valuation method from the characteristic given by putting a tick in the relevant column of the table below.

Characteristic	FIFO	LIFO	AVCO
• Where material prices are rising rapidly, jobs may show unrealistically high profits			
• Is of particular value where units of material are not separately definable			
• Material costs used are likely to be in line with other costs and prices			

Task 2.3

Identify the correct definitions by putting a tick into the relevant column of the table below.

Definition	Bin card	Stores Ledger Account	Purchase invoice
• Records quantity and value for each line of stock			
• Details the cost of stock bought and the date payment is due			
• Records quantities of stock received and issued and the balance in hand			

Task 2.4

Tiphook Ltd has the following movements in a certain type of stock into and out of it stores for the month of April:

DATE	RECEIPTS		ISSUES	
	Units	Cost	Units	Cost
April 1	150	£900		
April 15	400	£2,600		
April 22	350	£2,800		
April 27			500	
April 30	200	£1,300		

Complete the table below for the issue and closing stock values.

Method	Cost of Issue on 27 April	Closing Stock at 30 April
FIFO	£	£
LIFO	£	£
AVCO	£	£

Task 2.5

Magic Ltd pays a time-rate of £8 per hour to its direct labour for a standard 38 hour week. Any of the labour force working in excess of 38 hours is paid an overtime rate of £12 per hour.

Calculate the gross wage for the week for the two workers in the table below.

Worker	Hours Worked	Basic Wage	Overtime	Gross Wage
D Mooney	38 hours	£	£	£
A Bhardwa	43 hours	£	£	£

Task 2.6

The following costs have been taken from the manufacturing accounts of Blythe Ltd.

	£
Opening stock of raw materials	14,000
Closing stock of raw materials	20,000
Opening stock of work in progress	16,000
Closing stock of work in progress	20,000
Opening stock of finished goods	60,000
Closing stock of finished goods	50,000
Purchases of raw materials	100,000
Direct labour	190,000
Manufacturing overheads	100,000

Use the information above to complete the table showing the costs for Blythe Ltd.

Cost	£
Direct Materials Used	
Prime Cost	
Factory Cost	
Factory Cost of Goods Manufactured	
Cost of Goods Sold	

Task 2.7

Identify the correct definitions by putting a tick into the relevant column of the table below.

Definition	Functional Budget	Income Statement	Cash Budget
• Used to determine future cash flows			
• Used, for example, to determine expected costs of production or levels of sales			
• Used to determine future profits			

Task 2.8

Complete the table below showing budgeted fixed costs, variable costs, total costs and unit cost at the different possible budgeted levels of production.

Units	Fixed costs	Variable costs	Total costs	Unit costs
150	£450	£375	£825	£5.50
300				
450				

Task 2.9

Passlow Ltd has produced a performance report detailing budgeted and actual cost for last month.

Calculate the amount of the variance for each cost type and then determine whether it is adverse or favourable by putting a tick in the relevant column of the table below.

Cost Type	Budget £	Actual £	Variance	Adverse	Favourable
Direct Materials	19,200	20,100	£		
Direct Labour	36,800	36,400	£		
Production Overheads	33,000	36,000	£		
Administration Overheads	23,000	27,400	£		
Selling and Distribution Overheads	21,000	20,900	£		

Task 2.10

Kyle Ltd has produced a performance report detailing budgeted and actual cost for last quarter. Any variance in excess of 5% of budget is deemed to be significant and should be reviewed.

Calculate the amount of the variance for each cost type and then determine whether it is significant or insignificant by putting a tick in the relevant column of the table below.

Cost Type	Budget £	Actual £	Variance	Significant	Not-significant
Direct Materials	15,000	16,000	£		
Direct Labour	42,000	44,000	£		
Production Overheads	30,000	32,000	£		
Administration Overheads	16,000	16,500	£		

Task 2.11

It was noted from the performance report for Maple Ltd for an earlier month that the following cost variances were significant:

- Direct material cost was lower as a result of less wastage from using better materials

- Direct labour costs were higher as workers took longer than expected to produce the items

These variances needed to be reported to the relevant managers for review and appropriate action if required. Identify from the list below a relevant manager for each significant variance to whom the performance report should be sent.

Variance	Manager
Direct Material Cost	
Direct Labour Cost	

List of potential managers to choose from:

- Sales manager
- Purchasing manager
- IT manager
- Chief accountant
- Production manager

Task 2.12

Identify the following statements as either true or false by putting a tick in the relevant column of the table below.

Statement	True	False
• Forecasting involves exercising control over aspects of the budget		
• Budgets are often used to motivate managers to perform in line with organisational plans		
• Only adverse variances need to be investigated		
• Budgets communicate plans to managers responsible for carrying them out		

Task 2.13

Winfrey Ltd has produced a performance report for last quarter, part of which appears below. Any variance in excess of 10% of budget is deemed to be significant and should be reviewed.

Calculate % variance for each cost type in the table below and determine whether they are significant.

Cost Type	Budget	Variance	% Variance	Significant	Not-significant
Direct Materials	£12,000	£900			
Direct Labour	£40,000	£4,100			
Production Overheads	£25,000	£3,000			
Administration Overheads	£9,000	£720			

Task 2.14

Khan Ltd has produced a performance report for last quarter, part of which appears below.

Determine what the actual costs were for each cost type

Cost Type	Budget	Variance	Adverse / Favourable	Actual cost
Direct Materials	£12,000	5%	Adverse	£
Direct Labour	£40,000	4%	Favourable	£
Production Overheads	£25,000	7%	Favourable	£
Administration Overheads	£9,000	3%	Adverse	£

KAPLAN PUBLISHING

2 Mock Assessment Answers

SECTION 1

Task 1.1

- Cost unit
- Cost centre
- Cost unit
- Cost centre

Task 1.2

- Material
- Overhead
- Overhead
- Labour

Task 1.3

- Direct
- Indirect
- Direct
- Indirect

Task 1.4

- False
- False
- True

Task 1.5

- A200
- A100
- B100
- C200
- B200

Task 1.6

- Production Cost
- Selling and Distribution Cost
- Production Cost
- Administration Cost

Task 1.7

- Variable
- Fixed
- Variable
- Fixed

Task 1.8

- Variable
- Variable
- Fixed
- Semi-variable

Task 1.9

- False
- True
- False
- True

Task 1.10

Element	Total Cost	Unit Cost
Materials	£60,000	£4.00
Labour	£90,000	£6.00
Overheads	£63,300	£4.22
Total	£213,300	£14.22

Task 1.11

- 300/200
- 400/100
- 100/100
- 400/100
- 200/100
- 200/200

Task 1.12

Element	Unit Cost
Materials	£2.40
Labour	£3.00
Overheads	£2.20
Total	£7.60

SECTION 2

Task 2.1

- False
- True
- True
- False

Task 2.2

- FIFO
- AVCO
- LIFO

Task 2.3

- Stores Ledger Account
- Purchase invoice
- Bin card

Task 2.4

Method	Issue Cost	Closing Stock
FIFO	£3,175	£4,425
LIFO	£3,775	£3,825
AVCO	£3,500	£4,100

Task 2.5

Worker	Hours Worked	Basic Wage	Overtime	Gross Wage
D Mooney	38	£304	£0	£304
A Bhardwa	43	£304	£60	£364

Task 2.6

Cost	£
Direct Materials Used	94,000
Prime Cost	284,000
Factory Cost	384,000
Factory Cost of Goods Manufactured	380,000
Cost of Goods Sold	390,000

Task 2.7

- Cash budget
- Functional budget
- Income statement

Task 2.8

Units	Fixed costs	Variable costs	Total costs	Unit costs
150	£450	£375	£825	£5.50
300	£450	£750	£1,200	£4
450	£450	£1,125	£1,575	£3.50

Task 2.9

Cost Type	Budget £	Actual £	Variance	Adverse	Favourable
Direct Materials	19,200	20,100	£900	√	
Direct Labour	36,800	36,400	£400		√
Production Overheads	33,000	36,000	£3,000	√	
Administration Overheads	23,000	27,400	£4,400	√	
Selling and Distribution Overheads	21,000	20,900	£100		√

Task 2.10

Cost Type	Budget £	Actual £	Variance	Significant	Not-significant
Direct Materials	15,000	16,000	£1,000	√	
Direct Labour	42,000	44,000	£2,000		√
Production Overheads	30,000	32,000	£2,000	√	
Administration Overheads	16,000	16,500	£500		√

Task 2.11

- Purchasing manager
- Production manager

Task 2.12

- False
- True
- False
- True

Task 2.13

Cost Type	Budget	Variance	% Variance	Significant	Not-significant
Direct Materials	£12,000	£900	7.5		√
Direct Labour	£40,000	£4,100	10.25	√	
Production Overheads	£25,000	£3000	12	√	
Administration Overheads	£9,000	£720	8		√

Task 2.14

Cost Type	Budget	Variance	Adverse / Favourable	Actual cost
Direct Materials	£12,000	5%	Adverse	£12,600
Direct Labour	£40,000	4%	Favourable	£38,400
Production Overheads	£25,000	7%	Favourable	£23,250
Administration Overheads	£9,000	3%	Adverse	£9,270

Note: Working backwards from a variance is, strictly speaking, off syllabus. However, it is worth seeing one example – just in case!

Direct materials – 5% adverse variance, so actual cost > budget

Actual cost = 105% × budget

Therefore budget = actual ÷ 1.05 = 12,600 ÷ 1.05 = 12,000

Production O/H – 7% favourable variance, so actual cost < budget.

Actual cost = 93% × budget

Therefore budget = actual ÷ 0.93 = 23,250 ÷ 0.93 = 25,000

KAPLAN PUBLISHING

INDEX

KAPLAN PUBLISHING